# Radical Love as Resistance

*Youth Participatory Action Research for Transformation*

Edited by Rachel Radina & Tammy Schwartz

Cover Design by Brian Taylor (IMGBAT, Ltd.)

# Contents

## Dedication

For Tom Dutton, a man of great integrity, wisdom, and radical love. You are a light when we find ourselves in dark places. You have inspired us with your life. Know, dearly missed friend, that your work lives on in all we do and aspire to be.

*This little light of mine, I'm going let it shine.*

# Acknowledgements

This book would not be possible without the partnerships that were built over the last 10 years. Building community takes time, and we are grateful for the folks who have engaged in this work with us. First, we would like to thank the youth for all of their work, persistence, and passion in the fight against injustice and inequity. You are the reason we continue in this work. Your spirit is contagious and fills us with hope and love.

We also want to thank our partner teachers who collaborated with our Urban Cohort students on the YPAR and also took part in writing pieces for the chapters. Without them, we could not do this work. Janet Albright-Willis, we are in awe of your passion, commitment and love for your students. You are a phenomenal teacher who fights for justice every day and embodies radical love. Andrea Spenny, we love witnessing your drive to stand up for what's right when it comes to your students. You go above and beyond to be a transformative educator who operates from a space of radical love. Aisha Rudolph-Nurredin, you create the space within school for your students to name what matters and to enact their agency for change. You embody what it means to be a teacher committed to her students. Heather Allentuck Davis, watching you grow into a teacher who fights for justice is a great joy. It is an even greater joy to watch the way you and your students resist what is wrong and fight for change.

Thank you to our current YPAR partner teachers who were not involved during the time of this project: Dr. Mary Webb, Deborah Williams, Andrea Brierly, and the awesome, Ms. Tasha.

Thank you to our past and current partner teachers who teach one of our Urban Cohort classes: Shirley Easley, Rodger Horton, Dr. Robin Cooper, Malaika Huey, Melissa Vennefron, and Dr. Ganiva Reyes.

We also want to thank our Urban Cohort students for engaging in this work and for writing chapters about the work they did alongside the youth. Your participation in this work of justice gives us hope for what schools can one day become.

Thank you to Michelle Wallace, who was a graduate student working with us at the time the book project began. She helped design and co-teach the class where the project started and provided mentorship and support to the students. We miss you dearly and hope that your current university understands how lucky they are to have you as part of their team. You are truly a transformative educator and someone who tirelessly fights for equity and justice. We love and miss our anchor!

Thank you to past and present graduate students who are an integral part of this work: Kevin Talbert, Jonathan Bennett, Hailee Gibbons, Emily Abrams, Phyllis Kyei Mensah, Brooke Norval, Savanna Kuertz, Shawna Obregon, Kiaya Carter, Jamie Viars, and Neelum Amin.

Thank you to Genesis Ross who was a graduate assistant in the program and is now currently co-teaching the first-year seminar. Your wisdom, calming presence, unwavering support and passion for creating change is inspiring, and we are lucky to have you on the team!

Thank you to the Urban Cohort students who have served as teaching assistants for the first-year seminar: Rob Cron, Christine Rose, Julianne Ballog, Amber Anderson, Tabitha Nolan, Skya Wright, Amber Greenwood, Leslie Jason, Cassidy Wilson, Maria Kahn, and Rachel Hollins.

Thank you to our current office goddess, Barb Ribbler, who takes care of the many logistical needs that make the program run. We couldn't do this without you!

Thank you to the folks at Peaslee Neighborhood Center: Jenn Arens, Jennifer Summers, Trish Richter, Larry Fogle, and Bebe Lacke. Thank you to our community mentors (past and present): Ms. June Alexander, Ms. Dorothy Darden, Ms. Elizabeth Burnside, Alicia Ferguson, Amy Silver, Jai Washington, Pat Youngblood, and LaGena Wilkins.

Thank you to Miami's Center for Community Engagement in Over-the-Rhine: Tom Dutton, former director and founder of the program, Bonnie Neumeier, John Blake, Dr. Chris Wilkey, and Alice Skirtz. You worked alongside community to create the foundation of what we do today.

Thank you to the folks at Community Matters in Lower Price Hill: Mary Delaney, Jenna Hippensteel, and Cynthia Ford. Although you were not a part of the work during this particular year, you are now an important partner, and we want to recognize your part in the current iteration of this work.

Thank you to the Miami University's Teacher Education department and special thanks to the following faculty who have been deeply involved in the work: Kim Wachenheim, Dr. Sheri Leafgren, Melissa Vennefron, Dr. Barb Rose, Dr. Naz Bautista, and Dr. Ganiva Reyes. We also want to thank Drs. Brittany Aronson and Lisa Weems from the Educational Leadership Department for their past and present involvement in the YPAR work.

Special thanks to our current department chair, Dr. Brian Schultz, for believing in and supporting this work.

Thank you to the Dean's office at Miami University who also continue to support our work. Special thanks to our current Dean, Dr. Michael Dantley, and Associate Dean, Dr. Denise Taliaferro Baszile, and to our former dean, Dr. Carine Feyten, who gave us the room to build and play in the sand box of teacher education transformation.

Special thanks to our former department chair and program consultant, Dr. Raymond Terrell. Not only did you plant the seeds for this work, but you wielded your administrative genius to water the garden.

We also need to thank the youth, teachers, scholars, educators, and activists who created the foundation for YPAR and who continue to engage in this important work. There are many scholars of color who we cite throughout this book, who have paved the way for others, and who we are immensely grateful to. As white women in the academy, we want to recognize that this powerful approach to pedagogy and research could not have happened without the direct engagement by folks who are experiencing the oppressive conditions that necessitate an approach such as YPAR. This powerful research methodology and pedagogy has come into existence through the experiences and theorizing of people of color. We engage in this work alongside teachers and students in the hopes that, together, we can work towards more just and equitable communities, fully knowing that whiteness and white supremacy lie at the root of many of the issues that exist in society.

We also want to thank our friends and families for their support. We could not do this work without them. I, Rachel, would like to thank my grandmother—without her support I know I would not be here today. She was one of the few people in my life who has ever truly seen me. I have never met a more loving, thoughtful, and beautiful human being. Although I lost my grandmother many years ago, she is always with me in spirit. She inspires me to be a better person and to fight for justice even when I am ready to give up. She taught me about love, compassion, and understanding, and I am forever grateful for her loving, powerful presence in my life. Thank you to the other strong women in my life who helped me be the person I am today: my mom Donna, my aunt Pam, and my sister Stephanie. And thank you to my nieces, Kaitlin and Brooklyn, and my nephew, Carlo. My family is the reason I do this work, and I hope they all know how much I love and appreciate them.

I, Tammy, would especially like to thank my deceased mom, Mary Hartman. This work, in part, grew out of your sacrifice and the ways you taught me to love and be generous without boundaries. Each time one of our youth mentors' eyes light up and they proclaim, "You mean I'm a kid and I can DO something?!" you live on. And, for my life partner, Steve Schwartz. When I come home tired at the end of each day, spent, you fill me with unconditional love and acceptance. You give me the nourishment to get back at the project of justice in its many forms. Every Tammy needs a Steve. Thank you, honey!

# Radical Love

Love is not an option, **radical love** is the only way forward.

Radical love does not ask permission,

it does not stand down when challenged,

it does not acquiesce because it's easier,

it does not smile when it needs to shout,

it does not waiver when tired,

it does not disappear when it's time to fight,

it does not water down its words and intentions,

it does not bow down to would-be oppressors,

it does not tremble when questioned,

it does not shut up and remain silent when asked to step down,

it does not sugarcoat lessons to make them easier to swallow,

it does not make nice with the oppressor,

it does not act as if words have no meaning or intention,

it does not apologize for being loud and present,

it does not ask to join the conversation,

it does not lay down to be rolled over and flattened,

it does not need to fit nicely into your framework,

it does not speak in such a way as to make you feel less threatened.

**Radical love** is an embodied state of being that refuses to be tamed, kept under chains, and locked away from the masses.

# Introduction

By Rachel Radina

## The Purpose of this Book

This book is a testament to the power of collaborative, liberatory approaches to research, curriculum, and pedagogy. As scholars, educators, and activists who work within a teacher education program, we believe that Youth Participatory Action Research (YPAR) is a tool that can be used to push back against the status quo within teacher education and K-12 schools. We know that there are other changes that need to occur at the policy level to combat the issues students are facing in schools and communities, but education can and does play a powerful role in the struggle for equity and justice. As Freire (2005) stated, "education is not the ultimate lever for social transformation, but without it transformation cannot occur" (p. 69). It is important for us to take collective action in all of the spaces where we have the power and privilege to do so and to model what this looks like for our students. We encourage our students to take on the roles of educator, activist, and scholar, but we do this alongside them, never expecting them to take this path on their own. Paulo Freire's concept of being co-learners in the process of a liberating education guides our work, as we realize that there can be no teaching without learning (Freire, 1998). Freire describes the relationship between teachers and students:

> *Through dialogue, the teacher-of-the-students and the students-of-the-teacher cease to exist and a new term emerges: teacher-student with student-teachers. The teacher is no longer merely the-one-who-teaches, but one who is himself taught in dialogue with the students, who in turn while being taught also teach.* (Freire, 1970, p. 80)

We aim to include this way of being with students both in college and K-12 classrooms, never assuming that we have all the answers and always leaving space for dialogue, critique, and reflection. We enter our classrooms and the communities in which we work with a sense of humbleness and respect for the students, youth, teachers, and many community partners who engage alongside us in this work with hope and passion. We do this collective work, grounded in radical love, knowing that we may not see the transformations in our communities we are working towards, but we are dedicated to struggle for a better tomorrow no matter the outcome. Part of the power of our collective work is in the process of being together in community and building relationships with one another in the service of love and justice. There are important and powerful things that happen along the way that cannot be planned for or mapped out.

As faculty members within the academy, we have access to resources and power to which college students, in-service teachers, community members, and youth in schools do not typically have access. We work to create spaces for collaboration with all of these stakeholders, and we try to share our power and resources toward collective goals. This is often a messy process, and in some ways, "we make the road by walking" (Horton & Freire, 1990, p. 6), but we cannot merely sit back and wait while injustice ravages our communities and schools. Therefore, we do this work, keeping our hearts and minds open to critique, knowing that there is always room for growth and improvement that will push us further in this journey. This book is a means of sharing our stories, our victories, and our challenges, so that other folks engaged in this powerful work or who hope to engage in this type of work might be inspired and to share the voices and action of the youth who were engaged in this process. We hope their stories of resistance inspire and propel others to take action. This book also adds to the growing body of literature on YPAR, which, as a research methodology, faces scrutiny and critique (Ayala et al., 2018; Cannella, 2008; Mirra, Garcia, & Morrell, 2016). As stated by scholars who engage with YPAR as a research methodology (e.g. Cammarota, 2016; Mirra, Garcia & Morrell, 2016), it is important that we write and publish about the work we are doing in order to push for change in regard to what is considered valuable research within the academy. Cammarota (2016) prompts educators to extend their thinking on the action component of YPAR by including documentation of the work "with the intention of perceiving the world as possibilities as opposed to problems" (p. 249). Ultimately, if, as a result of this effort, youth, community members, teachers, activists, college students, scholars, and educators share their knowledge and experience doing this important work, our collaborative efforts may extend beyond traditional boundaries and borders that have been created to separate us and keep us from growing in solidarity. YPAR is powerful in its own right, but we must also write about this work so that it reaches audiences both in and outside of the academy.

**Grounded in Radical Love**

Our work needs to be meaningful—this is heart work. It requires openness, courage, vulnerability, passion, a willingness to grow and to push forward when things are hard, to live in the discomfort, to work towards liberation—the liberation of ourselves and of all people. Anaïs Nin is said to have written this quote, "the time came when the risk to remain tight in a bud was more painful than the risk it took to blossom," beautifully expressing both the pain and the need for personal growth. In order to really do this work and to commit ourselves wholly, we must believe that our humanity and liberation are bound up with the humanity and liberation of others. As stated by Freire (1970), "Radicalization involves increased commitment to the position one has chosen, and thus ever greater engagement in the effort to transform concrete, objective reality" in regard to the oppressive conditions we see all around us (p. 37). We must also remember that resistance is not a one-time event—it's part of a constant struggle for liberation and social change (Kelley, Tuck, & Yang, 2014)—a way of being in the world as opposed to a means to an end.

To do this work grounded in radical love, requires expanding our thinking in regard to the meaning of love. We do not conceptualize love as a noun, but as a verb, an action that is fueled by our deepest hopes and dreams for a future that is yet to be. bell hooks (2000a) suggests that to "begin by always thinking of love as an action rather than a feeling is one way in which anyone using the word in this manner automatically assumes accountability and responsibility" (p. 13). Just as theory cannot be disconnected from practice, the theory of love is merely empty rhetoric without practice—"love is an action, a participatory emotion" (hooks, 2000a, p. 163). We need more love in this this world, but not a soft, flowery sense of love that makes us forget the pain we are experiencing, while trying to make sense of all this hate and oppression. Yes, we need that kind of love too, but this is about something else. We mean the kind of love that rises out of the struggle. The kind of love that erupts out of anger. The rage that bubbles up inside that can only do one of two things: tear us into pieces or propel us into action. Some days, we feel like we are being ripped to shreds on the inside by this rage and pain. But, on the days when that rage erupts as love, we begin to understand that we cannot be afraid to resist the hurt and the pain we see all around us. Resistance and taking a fighting stance in the struggle for liberation is the only way forward. As stated by Reyes, Radina, and Aronson (2018):

> Love ("armed loved"-Paulo Freire) exists in the cracks, seeping in and opening up space for resistance. Rather than acquiescing to the systemic oppression that marginalizes and neglects historically disenfranchised youth, we call on resistance as act of love. (p. 819)

This radical orientation to love is critical if we hope to work towards equity and justice in our schools and communities. As stated by Moh Hardin (2011):

> In the Buddhist tradition, love is an immense concept—larger perhaps, than our everyday thinking about it. Love is not just a feeling we have toward our spouse, our family, or our friends. It includes these relationships, of course, but love is a way of being present and awake in the world together. (p. 2)

Love requires us to "see the world the way it is" (hooks, 2000a, p. 33), not to despair and feel all hope is lost, but to see the world unveiled and seek to take collective action.

Love and understanding are intertwined (Nhat Hanh, 2007), so in order to love, we must understand one another, and in order to do that, we must build relationships with one another. bell hooks (2000b) states, "true love is rooted in recognition and acceptance, that love combines acknowledgment, care, responsibility, commitment, and knowledge, we understand there can be no love without justice" (p. 104). Work grounded in radical love requires us to take action. Engaging in radical love grounded in the need to take collective action requires courage, and "there is no better place to learn the art of loving than in community" (hooks, 2000a, p. 127). We must love in solidarity; "to love is to look at each other and to look together in the same direction" (Nhat Hanh, 2007, p. x). We must see one another and be willing to engage in the work of reaching a common goal—this is how we work from a space of radical love. hooks (2009) powerfully states:

> *It is the most militant, most radical intervention anyone can make to not only speak of love but to engage in the practice of love. For love as the foundation of all social movements for self-determination is the only way we create a world that domination and dominator thinking cannot destroy. Anytime we do the work of love, we are doing the work of ending domination.* (p. 248)

We have come to believe in the powerful conclusion "that human beings in communion liberate each other" (Freire, 1970, p. 133). We must engage in the work of radical self-love, and "we must learn to be with each other if we plan to get free" (Taylor, 2018, p. 73).

**What is Youth Participatory Action Research (YPAR)?**

Historically, research has been used as a tool to study and objectify people of color, including youth (Ayala et al., 2018). This approach to research has often perpetuated deficit-laden theories, particularly when the research has been conducted on youth of color and/or youth who are experiencing poverty (Rodríguez & Brown, 2009). YPAR, on the other hand, provides a space for youth to be researchers, focusing on their own lived experiences and grounded in their firsthand knowledge on the topic of study (Ayala et al., 2018; Radina et al., 2018). YPAR, as a research methodology, acts as a form of resistance against the oppressive, systemic conditions that often stifle and silence the power of youth (Irizarry & Brown, 2014). Given the liberatory goals of YPAR, it must always be research *with*, not *on*, youth (Guishard & Tuck, 2014). The humanizing, problem-posing approach of YPAR has the potential to transform oppressive conditions and liberate participants. Cammarota (2016) suggests that youth are attuned to the injustices they witness and experience in their communities through what Du Bois termed "second sight." This allows youth to understand how they are viewed by those in dominant social groups and how they view themselves outside of the gaze of those who define them as "other." However, although youth are aware of the injustice, they likely do not yet have the ability to identify the system as the source of injustice and oppression. It is only "through praxis that young people of color transform second sight into critical consciousness" (Cammarota, 2016, p. 234). Coming to critical consciousness is a goal in and of itself within the YPAR process and youth who begin to understand the conditions of their schools and communities as part of an unjust social order may feel more inclined to take action to change those conditions.

YPAR stems from Participatory Action Research (PAR) and is rooted in the grassroots and change movements that pushed for the full participation of those experiencing oppression (Cahill, 2007; Irizarry, 2009; Irizarry & Brown, 2014). YPAR is defined by Mirra, Garcia, and Morrell (2016) as

> *the practice of mentoring young people to become social scientists by engaging them in all aspects of the research cycle, from developing research questions and examining relevant literature to collecting and analyzing data and offering findings about social issues that they find meaningful and relevant.* (p. 2)

This method of research was inspired by Paulo Freire as a mode of consciousness-raising and helps participants understand their inherent power to make change (Ayala et al., 2018; Foster-Fishman, Law, Lichty, & Aoun, 2010). Grounded in Freire's (1970) concept of "the pedagogy of the oppressed, a pedagogy that must be forged *with*, not *for*, the oppressed" (p. 48), youth are able to see themselves as part of the struggle for liberation alongside other partners in the YPAR work. YPAR bridges the gap between the lived realities of students and the classroom curriculum (Cammarota & Romero, 2011; Irizarry, 2009). It gives students the tools to push back against institutional, social, and political conditions that have contributed to personal and community issues (Wang, Morrel-Samuels, Hutchinson, Bell, & Pestronk, 2004). According to Cammarota and Fine (2008), "young people resist the normalization of systematic oppression by understanding their own engaged praxis—critical and collective inquiry, reflection, and action focused on 'reading' and speaking back to the reality of the world, their world" (pp. 1-2). YPAR moves beyond traditional ways of conducting research by: (1) taking a collective approach to the research; (2) utilizing the lived experience of the youth; (3) centering the intersection of identities (e.g. race, social class, gender, sexual orientation); (4) seeking to gain knowledge that challenges the status quo; and (5) being active as opposed to passive (Cammarota & Fine, 2008). As powerfully stated by Irizarry (2009), "YPAR challenges the traditional roles of youth as passive recipients of education and consumers of knowledge by repositioning them as active learners and knowledge producers" (p. 197). It is through this type of curriculum, pedagogy, and research that students can use their voices to push for change in their classrooms and communities.

## Why we Chose to use YPAR as Pedagogy and as a Research Methodology

Currently, as a nation, we often claim that every child in the United States has access to a free, public education. We take pride in this notion and falsely proclaim that this supposed access to education sets a level playing field for success and the attainment of the "American Dream." We continue to uphold the idea of meritocracy and project a narrative that suggests that being a smart, hardworking, good (i.e. obedient) citizen is all that is necessary for success. However, many know that the quality of education a child receives depends heavily upon their positionality (i.e. social class, race, ethnicity, home language, gender, sexual orientation). Critical scholars continue to point out that schools create a hegemonic space in which certain students (i.e. white, middle class, straight, able-bodied, cisgender, men) are given cultural dominance over all other students (Howard, 2006; Irizarry, 2009; Irizarry & Brown, 2014; Ladson-Billings, 2001; Milner 2010). In urban contexts, race and social class create a situation in which students of color and students experiencing poverty, in order to succeed in school, are forced to assimilate into a hegemonic culture that fails to recognize them or their culture as legitimate (Alim & Paris, 2017; Chou & Tozer, 2008; Fordham, 1996; Ladson-Billings, 2000). As stated by Milner (2010):

> *Standardization, in many ways, is antithetical to diversity because it suggests that all students live and operate in homogeneous environments with equality of opportunity afforded to them.* (p. 3)

Schools of education must work to create culturally relevant educators who push back against these oppressive conditions in schools and instead create communities of learning based on equity and justice. Valenzuela (2016) states that "education is about people. It is about how we as individuals and as members of moral communities move and get on in the world" (p. 6). Critical educators must use curriculum and pedagogy that confront these issues head-on and create educational practices that inspire, transform, and reimagine—Youth Participatory Action Research (YPAR) has this potential.

YPAR is a powerful curriculum tool that taps into more critical forms of teaching, such as culturally relevant and multicultural pedagogies (Irizarry, 2009). In addition, students learn skills and competencies directly related to research, writing, reading, math, and more (Irizarry & Brown, 2014). YPAR provides tools that educators can use in the classroom to help facilitate deep discussions with youth about the social issues that cause inequity, as well as provide youth space in which to voice concerns about these issues and take action (Cammarota, 2017). In order for students to see themselves as potential agents of change, as radical resistors, they must first develop critical consciousness, what Freire (1970) referred to as "conscientização" (p. 67). YPAR provides a method of developing critical consciousness, and through lifting the veil, students clearly see systemic oppression and also see themselves as part of the struggle for liberation (Cammarota, 2016). Similar to other YPAR practitioners, we aim "to have youth develop a powerful personal narrative of themselves as caring and capable community change agents" (Burke, Greene, & McKenna, 2017, p. 587). Too often, academia seeks to keep the ideas of resistance confined to the realm of theory—docile and unmoving—a mere descriptor with no possibility for creating social change. However, "educators have a shared responsibility to ensure our youth have the ability to participate in society as democratic citizens, enlivened by the power of resistance to create meaningful social change" (Radina, 2013, p. 179). YPAR provides a link between the academy and the classroom, as well as the classroom and the community. Many youth face inequities in their daily lives and often believe they have no power to change these realities (Rodríguez & Brown, 2009). YPAR provides the critical tools needed to help youth see the power they already possess and to understand how they might use it in their own lives and communities (Ayala et al., 2018; Cammarota & Fine, 2008; Irizarry & Brown, 2014). It is imperative that we work alongside youth instead of for them, and YPAR provides the theory and practice to do so. This is a dream and possibility for public education that has not yet reached its full potential.

YPAR provides a space to push back against systems of injustice. It's a powerful approach to pedagogy and research because it taps into the inherent power that indigenous folks possess to fight for their own liberation. As stated by Mirra et al., (2016), "the most revolutionary aspect of YPAR is the realization of the full humanity of young people" (p. 4). Scholars have pointed out that there are some people within the research community that are critical of YPAR and think it is less rigorous and accurate than other forms of research (Ayala et al., 2018; Cannella, 2008; Mirra et al., 2016). However, for practitioners who plan to do this kind of work, it's important to keep in mind that any type of research that questions the status quo and the current power dynamics will be seen as dangerous by those who wish to uphold traditional research paradigms that privilege white supremacist, capitalist heteropatriarchy. As stated by Rodríguez and Brown (2009), YPAR is "explicitly political" in nature and, thus, "is an ideal methodology for engaging marginalized youth in educational transformation" (p. 24). YPAR faces scrutiny, in large part, because it is powerful, and the main goal is to take action against issues of injustice and inequity. Those in power understand that "when you control a man's thinking you do not have to worry about his actions" (Woodson, 1933/2010, p. 15). YPAR threatens the status quo because it raises the consciousness of youth, disrupting the hegemonic narratives that have led many youths to believe that academic "failure" is due to individual deficits and not systemic forms of oppression (Coburn & Gormally, 2017; Rodríguez & Brown, 2009). It also positions youth "as part of the active present" and not merely pawns in a society that is already created for them (Kelley et al., 2014, p. 92). Youth have the power to imagine new possibilities and work towards the creation of a future society that is more equitable and just.

While many research paradigms and projects position indigenous folks as the objects of study, YPAR positions them as the subjects (Duncan-Andrade & Morrell, 2008; Irizarry & Brown, 2014) or "partners in the inquiry process" (Cammarota, Berta-Ávila, Ayala, Rivera, & Rodríguez, 2016, p. 69). This creates more liberatory possibilities and stands in stark contrast to traditional notions of who gets to produce knowledge. Scholars such as Duncan-Andrade and Morrell (2008) promote the inclusion of YPAR in teacher education programs as a viable approach to curriculum and pedagogy. We have sought to include YPAR in our Teacher Preparation curriculum by adding it into our Urban Cohort Program, which primarily prepares teachers to work in urban schools. As we continue this work, we hope to bring this approach to curriculum, pedagogy, and research into the general teacher education program.

**Who is Involved in the Work?**

One of the overarching goals of YPAR is to include multiple populations of people who are typically left out of the research process (Duncan-Andrade & Morrell, 2008). Our work includes an intergenerational, multiracial group of people who care about similar things—in-service teachers, pre-service teachers, youth, community members and university faculty. Our Urban Cohort Program was previously dedicated to the preparation of teachers, but over the last few years, the program has expanded and become more interdisciplinary. Now, we not only prepare teachers to work in urban schools, but we prepare an array of professions (social workers, public health professionals, psychologists, etc.) who are interested in better understanding urban contexts.

The undergraduate students involved in the Urban Cohort Program take part in a year-long seminar (see the next chapter for a full description of program). There is a service component attached to the seminar, and each Urban Cohort student is assigned to one of our four partner schools. Two of the teachers at our partner schools, Andrea Spenny & Heather Allentuck Davis, are graduates of the Urban Cohort Program. Our collaborating teacher at Urban Elementary, Janet Albright-Willis, is a longtime partner and was involved in the pilot of the YPAR component of the program during the 2014-2015 school year. (Note: to shield the privacy of our youth mentors, all school names have been replaced with pseudonyms.)

The collaborating teachers at each partner school recruit students to be youth mentors in the YPAR program. We intentionally work to flip the power dynamics of traditional mentoring relationships by making the youth the mentors and the college students the mentees. This does not mean that the relationship isn't reciprocal, but it sets the stage for helping the youth in the program to understand their own inherent power to make change in their communities and schools. We also know that there are still power dynamics at play due to age, social class, race and other important factors. As stated by Irizarry & Brown (2014),

> while power cannot be completely equalized, PAR researchers work toward this ideal and work to ensure that power is not used in suppressive or coercive ways—that is, that power is used "with" and not "over" others. (p. 65)

This is one step we are taking to try and even out the power dynamics and center the experiences and knowledge of the youth in the program. As we move forward with this work, we will continue to look for ways to soften traditional power dynamics that tend to get in the way of the work.

The college students, the youth mentors, the collaborating teachers, and the faculty members involved in the program met at Peaslee Neighborhood Center in Over-the-Rhine one Saturday a month and two Fridays a semester at one of our four partner schools over the course of one academic year. On the Saturdays, the youth mentors and mentees spent four hours engaging in relationship building activities, discussing social justice, and conducting/planning the research in the later stages of the program. This is described in more detail in the chapters dedicated to each school. The two Fridays that the mentees spent at their partner schools provided time to further build relationships with the youth mentors and shadow them during the school day. This was also beneficial for the college students who plan to teach upon graduation because they were able to spend time in urban classrooms with their youth mentors as guides with first-hand knowledge. At some of the schools, the youth mentors and mentees got to spend some of their time working on their YPAR projects, but the bulk of the time on these Fridays was spent shadowing the youth mentors.

## Chapter Authors & the Organization of the Book

The chapters in this book are co-authored by the Urban Cohort students who took part in each YPAR group, our partner teachers, and the volume's editors. At the beginning of the project, we were hoping to have the youth mentors co-write the chapters as well. Unfortunately, due to the time constraints of the Urban Cohort students and the ending of the school year, we were not able to make this happen. For future projects, we will be more intentional about making sure the youth have the opportunity to be co-authors. Even though the youth did not co-author the book chapters, you will see some of their writing, projects, pictures, etc. The college students in the Urban Cohort Program had collective class readings and readings that were uniquely designed by the course instructors, Rachel Radina and Michelle Wallace, to be specific to the topics and/or contexts of each groups' YPAR work. Students in the class were tasked with writing book chapters about their YPAR work grounded in their experiences with the youth and their in-class readings as the final project for the second semester of their first-year seminar.

The first chapter of the book describes the Urban Cohort program and provides some information about two of our long-time partners, Peaslee Neighborhood Center and Miami University's Center for Community Engagement in Over-the-Rhine. The chapter ends with a description of Over-the-Rhine, one of the neighborhoods where the YPAR work takes place. This is a neighborhood that is in the late stages of gentrification, and the community continues to lose vital social services and other community assets. This chapter is included at the beginning of the book because it's important that we contextualize the work before moving onto the chapters that specifically address the YPAR work.

Chapter 2 was written by five of the Urban Cohort students about their YPAR project with the youth mentors from Urban STEM School. Their YPAR project was focused on bullying in their school, and so all of their class readings were about bullying, which included Dillon's (2012), No Place for Bullying: Leadership for Schools that Care for Every Student. Three of our four partner teachers wrote introductions to the Urban Cohort student-authored book chapters included in this book. Aisha Rudolph-Nurredin was not able to contribute an intro to the chapter written about the work that took place at Urban STEM school, but she was an integral part of the project the Urban Cohort students and their youth mentors collaborated on within her classroom. She ensured that her students were able to create a mural within her school, helped the students facilitate a parent night to inform families and other students about bullying, helped them create a play on bullying, which they were later able to perform, and also made possible the data collection discussed in the book chapter on bullying in their school. Aisha identifies as a Black woman and has been teaching in urban schools for many years.

The introduction to Chapter 3 was written by Andrea Spenny, our partner teacher at MLK High School. Andrea is a graduate from Miami University and the Urban Cohort program. Andrea is a high school English teacher and has been teaching at MLK High School for 4 years. She identifies as a white, middle class woman. Chapter 3 was co-written by Andrea and five of the Urban Cohort students about the YPAR project they collaborated on with their youth mentors researching school discipline. Their readings were focused on this topic. They were also assigned to read From Education to Mass Incarceration: Dismantling the School-to-Prison Pipeline by Nocella, Parmar, and Stovall (2014). As can happen with YPAR, their project started off focusing on school discipline but later focused on personal growth and leadership.

Heather Allentuck Davis wrote the introduction to Chapter 4 and is also a graduate of Miami University and the Urban Cohort. Heather has been working as a middle school teacher in urban schools for the past five years teaching math. She was interested in being involved in the YPAR work to empower students and pre-service teachers to see themselves as valued members of and agents of change within their communities. She also believes it allows her to be a better teacher through listening and building relationships, leading her to create more relevant and impactful learning experiences. Heather identifies as a white, middle class female. The chapter was co-written by Heather and four Urban Cohort students. The chapter describes the YPAR work that took place with the youth mentors, and their topic of focus was community violence, which later transitioned to building a better community. Their assigned book, Alexander's (2010), The New Jim Crow: Mass Incarceration in the Age of Colorblindness, centered on systemic violence, particularly the criminal justice system.

Janet Albright Willis wrote the introduction to Chapter 5. She has been a part of the YPAR program from the beginning and is the partner teacher from Urban Elementary. She is an intervention specialist at Urban Elementary School and lives in the community where she teaches. She has been teaching in urban schools for twenty years. She earned her undergraduate degree from Xavier University in Cincinnati, and her Master of Education degree from Antioch University in Yellow Springs, Ohio. Her greatest joy in engaging in this work is being able to experience the birth of renewed young voices for just causes and to witness their engagement. Janet also teaches university classes in order to help prepare pre-service teachers for the classroom. She identifies as a Black female. Chapter 5 was co-written by Janet and six Miami students. The focus of their YPAR work was originally poverty and then later the students decided to focus on food insecurity. Their book was focused on the neighborhood context of Over-the-Rhine, which is the location of our longest school partnership. They were assigned Skirtz's (2012), Econocide: Elimination of the Urban Poor. This book was written by a local social worker, Alice Skirtz, who has been a part of the community for many years as both a practitioner and an activist. She tells the story of the history of struggle in Over-the-Rhine and what led to the current state of the neighborhood, which has been completely changed due to gentrification.

The final chapter concludes the book and delves into the connection between radical love, resistance, and the YPAR work, which we ultimately hope leads to both personal and collective transformation.

# References

Alexander, M. (2010). *The new Jim Crow: Mass incarceration in the age of colorblindness.* New York, NY: New Press.

Alim, H. S., & Paris, D. (2017). What is culturally sustaining pedagogy and why does it matter? In D. Paris & H. S. Alim (Eds.), *Culturally sustaining pedagogies: Teaching and learning for justice in a changing world* (pp. 67-89). New York, NY: Teachers College Press.

Ayala, J., Cammarota, J., Berta-Ávila, M. I., Rivera, M., Rodríguez, L. F., & Torre, M. E. (2018). *Par entremundos: A pedagogy of the Américas.* New York, NY: Peter Lang.

Burke, K. J., Greene, S., & McKenna, M. K. (2017). Youth voice, civic engagement and failure in participatory action research. *Urban Review, 49,* 585-601.

Cahill, C. (2007). Doing research with young people: Participatory research and the rituals of collective work. *Children's Geographies, 5*(3), 297-312.

Cammarota, J. (2016). The praxis of ethnic studies: Transforming second sight into critical consciousness. *Race Ethnicity and Education, 19*(2), 233-251.

Cammarota, J. (2017). Youth participatory action research: A pedagogy of transformational resistance for critical youth studies. *Journal for Critical Education Policy Studies, 15*(2), 188-213.

Cammarota, J., Berta-Ávila, M., Ayala, J., Rivera, M., & Rodríguez, L. (2016). PAR entremundos: A practitioner's guide. In A. Valenzuela (Ed.), *Growing critically conscious teachers: A social justice curriculum for educators of Latino/a youth* (pp. 67-89). New York, NY: Teachers College Press.

Cammarota, J., & Fine, M. (2008). *Revolutionizing education: Youth participatory action research in motion.* New York, NY: Routledge.

Cammarota, J., & Romero, A. (2011). Participatory action research for high school students: Transforming, policy, practice, and the personal with social justice education. *Educational Policy, 25*(3), 488-506.

Cannella, C. M. (2014). Faith in process, faith in people: Confronting policies of social disinvestment with PAR as pedagogy for expansion. In J. Cammarota & M. Fine (Eds.), *Revolutionizing education: Youth participatory action research in motion* (pp. 189-212). New York, NY: Routledge.

Chou, V., & Tozer, S. (2008). What's urban got to do with? The meanings of urban in urban teacher preparation and development. In F. P. Peterman (Ed.), *Partnering to prepare urban teachers: A call to activism* (pp. 1-20). New York, NY: Peter Lang.

Coburn, A., & Gormally, S. (2017). *Communities for social change: Practicing equality and social justice in youth and community work.* New York, NY: Peter Lang.

Dillon, J. (2012). *No place for bullying: Leadership for schools that care for every student.* Thousand Oaks, CA: Corwin.

Duncan-Andrade, J. M. R., & Morrell, E. (2008). *The art of critical pedagogy: Possibilities for moving from theory to practice in urban schools.* New York, NY: Peter Lang.

Fordham, S. (1996). *Blacked out: Dilemmas of race, identity, and success at Capital High*. Chicago, IL: The University of Chicago Press.

Foster-Fishman, P., Law, K., Lichty, L., & Aoun, C. (2010). Youth reACT for social change: A method for youth participatory action research. *American Journal of Community Psychology, 46*(1/2), 67-83.

Freire, P. (1970). *Pedagogy of the oppressed*. New York, NY: Continuum.

Freire, P. (1998). *Pedagogy of freedom, ethics, democracy, and civic courage*. Lanham, MD: Rowan & Littlefield Publishers.

Freire, P. (2005). *Teachers as cultural workers: Letters to those who dare teach*. Boulder, CO: Westview Press.

Guishard, M., & Tuck, E. (2014). Youth resistance research methods and ethical challenges. In E. Tuck & K. W. Yang (Eds.), *Youth resistance research and theories of change* (pp.181-194). New York, NY: Routledge.

Hardin, m. (2011). *A little book of love: Buddhist wisdom on bringing happiness to ourselves and our world*. Boston, MA: Shambhala Publications, Inc.

hooks, b. (2000a). *All about love: New visions*. New York, NY: HarperCollins Inc.

hooks, b. (2000b). *Feminism is for everybody: Passionate politics*. Cambridge, MA: Southend Press.

hooks, b. (2009). Lorde: The imagination of justice. In R. P. Byrd, J. Betsch Cole, & B. Guy-Sheftall (Eds.), *I am your sister: Collected and unpublished writings of Audre Lorde* (pp. 242-248). New York, NY: Oxford University Press.

Horton, M., & Freire, P. (1990). *We make the road by walking*. Philadelphia, PA: Temple University Press.

Howard, G. R. (2006). *We can't teach what we don't know: White teachers, multiracial schools*. New York, NY: Teachers College Press.

Irizarry, J. G. (2009). Reinvigorating multicultural education through youth participatory action research. *Multicultural Perspectives, 11*(4), 194-199.

Irizarry, J. G., & Brown, T. M. (2014). Humanizing research in dehumanizing spaces: The challenges and opportunities of conducting participatory action research with youth in schools. In D. Paris & M. Winn (Eds.), *Humanizing research: Decolonizing qualitative inquiry with youth and communities* (pp. 63-80). Thousand Oaks, CA: Sage Publications

Kelley, R. D. G., Tuck, E., & Yang, K. W. (2014). Resistance as revelatory. In E. Tuck & K. W. Yang (Eds.), *Youth resistance research and theories of change* (pp. 82-96). New York, NY: Routledge.

Ladson-Billings, G. (2000). Fighting for our lives: Preparing teachers to teach African American students. *Journal of Teacher Education, 51*(3), 206-214.

Ladson-Billings, G. (2001). *Crossing over to Canaan: The journey of new teachers in diverse classrooms*. San Francisco, CA: Josey-Bass.

Milner, H. R., IV. (2010). *Understanding diversity, opportunity gaps, and teaching in today's classrooms. Start where you are but don't stay there.* Cambridge, MA: Harvard Education Press.

Mirra, N., Garcia, A., & Morrell, E. (2016). *Doing youth participatory action research: Transforming inquiry with researchers, educators and students.* New York, NY: Routledge.

Nhat Hanh, T. (2007). *Teachings on love.* Berkeley, CA: Parallax Press.

Nocella, A. J., Parmar, P. & Stovall, D. (Eds.). (2014). *From education to mass incarceration: Dismantling the school-to-prison pipeline.* New York, NY: Peter Lang.

Radina, R. (2013). Student protest: Blind ignorance of empowering curriculum? In T. S. Poetter (Ed.) *Curriculum windows: What curriculum theorists of the 1960s can teach us about schools and society today* (pp. 165-180). Charlotte, NC: Information Age Publishing.

Radina, R., Schwartz, T., Ross, G., Aronson, B., Albright-Willis, J., Wallace, M., & Norval, B. (2018). A space for us too: Using youth participatory action research to center youth voices. *School-University-Community Partnerships, 11*(4), 122-139.

Reyes, G., Radina, R., & Aronson, B. (2018). Teaching against the grain as an act of love: Disrupting white Eurocentric masculinist frameworks within teacher education. *The Urban Review, 50,* 818-835.

Rodríguez, L. F., & Brown, T. M. (2009). From voice to agency: Guiding principles for participatory action research with youth. *New Directions for Youth Development, 123,* 19-34.

Skirtz, A. (2012). *Econocide: Elimination of the urban poor.* Washington, DC: NASW Press.

Taylor, S. R. (2018). *The body is not an apology: The power of radical self-love.* Oakland, CA: Berrett-Koehler Publishers, Inc.

Valenzuela, A. (2016). *Growing critically conscious teachers. A social justice curriculum for educators of Latino/a youth.* New York, NY: Teachers College Press.

Wang, C. C., Morrel-Samuels, S., Hutchison, P. M., Bell, L., & Pestronk, R. M. (2004). Fling photovoice: Community building among youths, adults, and policymakers. *American Journal of Public Health, 94*(6), 911-913.

Woodson, C. G. (2010). *The miseducation of the negro.* Las Vegas: IAP. (Original work published 1933)

# I Am:

## Black Lives Matter

(A stem poem based on the work of Julio Cammarota)
**By Aleah J. Holley**

I am angry and hopeful
I wonder when they will care
I hear the rejoicing bells of liberation
I see the mothers cry
I want love to conquer
I am angry and hopeful

I pretend that I am okay
I feel the sun lifting us up
I touch the comfort of clouds
I worry they will not be able to protect us
I cry because of the injustice
I am angry and hopeful

I understand we must keep working
I say we shall overcome
I dream that Black Lives Matter
I try to be patient
I hope the bells ring and the sun shines down
I am angry and hopeful

# Chapter 1: The Urban Cohort & The Context of the Work

By Rachel Radina & Tammy Schwartz

## Miami University Urban Cohort

Figure 1: The 2016-2017 Cohort

The Urban Cohort (UC) was originally designed to supplement the general undergraduate teacher education program at Miami University and to specifically prepare teachers to be culturally relevant educators in urban schools and communities. Prior to its official conception, leaders in our college planted the seeds for this work as they engaged across our Educational Leadership and Teacher Education Departments to find a way to better prepare our students to teach in urban schools. In particular, Dr. Michael Dantley, then the Chair for the Educational Leadership Department, and Dr. Raymond Terrell, Assistant Dean for Diversity, championed the work in this area. As men of color who were both formerly principals in urban schools, they witnessed the discrepancies between what teacher preparation, particularly at a predominantly white institution (PWI), was doing to critically engage teacher candidates around issues of race, equity, education, and social justice and what was needed to have systemic impact in urban schools. We are forever grateful for their seeds, love, passion, determination, and commitment that paved the way for our team to move forward. Since our early days, we have expanded into an interdisciplinary program but still primarily attract teacher education majors. The program prompts students to interrogate their own power and privilege and to see themselves as potential agents of social change who advocate for social justice *alongside* youth and other community members. This program is housed in a PWI with a student culture that leads to many challenges around race, social class, gender, sexuality, ability, and nationality. The university is a microcosm of society, and thus, given the ideology of white supremacist heteropatriarchy that permeates the United States, it is not surprising that this ideology and other forms of oppression show up within the context of our university. It is also an institution that attracts middle to upper class students. The school has been nicknamed a "Public Ivy" and, as a result of this association, there are also issues that arise due to social class on our campus. The UC program has historically been a space that attracts students who have felt that they are somehow on the margins on our campus. It is also a program that attracts white students who want to make a difference in urban communities and schools, but these students, like all of white America, need to figure out what Martin Luther King, Jr. (1968) calls the "significant price" one is willing to pay to understand the harm caused by white supremacy and to eradicate injustice (p. 12). Part of the role our program plays is disrupting "white savior" narratives that have historically attracted white teachers into teaching in urban schools (Sato & Lensmire, 2009). While engaging our students in pedagogies to deepen racial literacy (Flynn, Rolon-Dow, & Worden, 2018), we seek to disrupt stereotypical depictions of urban schools, communities, and students. This is important when preparing pre-service teachers because, as bell hooks (2003) points out:

> *Teachers are often among that group most reluctant to acknowledge the extent to which white-supremacist thinking informs every aspect of our culture including the way we learn, the content of what we learn, and the manner in which we are taught.* (p. 25)

We also firmly believe that "poverty is a social condition created by the decisions of the powerful" and has nothing to do with perceived deficits of individuals (Ladson-Billings, 2017, p. 82). As scholars and educators who primarily work in the field of teacher education, we take seriously our role in working towards the eradication of oppression in all of the many forms it exists, both in and outside of schools. We also realize that some of the identities and ways we show up reinforce systems of oppression and that we must constantly be critically self-reflective and mindful of our own positionalities and the power dynamics that come along with them. We know that these same oppressive realities show up within our program, and we work hard to lessen these conditions, knowing that we cannot fully eradicate them. Many of the folks who are deeply involved in this work (including the editors of this book and our students) unapologetically critique and give feedback in order to make our program stronger and more grounded in principles of equity and justice. Given the nature of our work, it is important that we position ourselves before further discussing the components of the program.

I, Rachel, identify as a white, queer, working-class, cisgender woman who was pushed out of school. As a student who experienced being pushed out of school, I am dedicated to being part of the work to create educational spaces that confirm and support all students in all the ways they show up. I am a teacher-educator because I want to help students see the value in becoming culturally relevant practitioners who center social justice in their classrooms and other professional contexts. I believe in the transformative potential in educational spaces that take a critical approach to knowledge and knowledge production, and through my own pedagogy and curriculum, I hope to inspire pre-service teachers to take up the call to create a more liberatory approach to education that is grounded in the lives, hopes, and dreams of their future students. I have a ton of unearned privilege, and I know I must critically reflect upon how that impacts the way I experience and navigate the world. I try to model this practice for my students, and I am often vulnerable in the classroom, even when I am afraid or uncomfortable. Doing critical social justice work requires vulnerability and showing up with our whole selves. This is not easy, and some days are more challenging than others, but if we are asking our students to do this, we must be willing to do this as well. Despite my efforts and best intentions, I know there are inevitably still times when I do harm in the space of my classroom, "because in a culture of domination almost everyone engages in behaviors that contradict their beliefs and values" (hooks, 2003, p. 29). This is especially true for white people, given that we live in a society dominated by white supremacy. I do not take this realization lightly, and I work hard to critically self-reflect and listen to the critiques and advice of colleagues, friends, and comrades.

I, Tammy, identify as a white, heterosexual, cisgender, and now, middle class woman with Appalachian roots. I am the daughter of a high school pushout, who at 16 married my father because of my impending birth. At age five, my father left. By that time, my mother had my sister and brother. After my father left, we spent a period of time couch surfing in different homes and apartments of friends and family, never knowing when the door would be closed because we had worn out our welcome. While struggling through a history of poverty, I am acutely aware that, despite my own pain, trauma, internalized shame, and material deprivation, my lived experience is NOTHING compared to the experiences of my peers of color. I sit with this everyday as a white person who now engages in this endeavor and as a former teacher in one of the neighborhoods in which we now work. As the director of this program, I fight for the soul of this work in the context of white supremist, neoliberal policies impacting higher education and the consumption of those policies in multiple spaces. In doing this, I work hard to continually hold myself accountable for justice and to engage in deep and uncomfortable conversations with my colleagues and students in and out of our UC program. This is not always easy, and I mess up a lot.

Students within the Urban Cohort program are also asked to interrogate their own positionalities and to understand how who they are in the world impacts their access to power and privilege and on what levels they experience oppression. In addition, teacher education students within our program are encouraged to understand that teaching is not only confined to the classroom, but that teachers should conceptualize themselves as "community teachers" (Murrell, 2001), "public professionals" (Klein, Taylor, Onore, Strom, & Abrams, 2013), and "community practitioners" (Longo, 2007). Teacher Education students are urged to consider that teachers should be concerned with what happens both in and outside of the classroom and seek to become community members in the neighborhoods in which they work. The program is a place-based approach to teacher education and centers the knowledge and experiences of our various community and school partners. Students in our program learn by doing and engage in a variety of immersive experiences that tap into the embodied ways in which we learn. We believe that transformative learning requires that we expand our classrooms beyond the walls of the university and tap into the wealth of community, family, and school resources that bring life to the curriculum we try to teach in our classrooms. We also hope this approach to education, embedded in the community, will impact the classrooms of the teacher education students we work alongside, helping them to become culturally relevant educators.

**Components of the UC Program**

In order to take part in the UC program, students must go through a rigorous application and screening process that is aimed at filling the program with students who hold certain dispositions or are open to new ways of knowing and knowledge production. This is done through an initial online screening process and application, followed by an in-depth interview with various key program stakeholders (e.g. community members, collaborating teachers, UC faculty, and students). Once students are accepted into the program, they participate in a variety of seminars, field experiences (e.g. urban immersions, service-learning projects, action research), and mentoring experiences as described below. The Urban Cohort is a 3-year program that provides them with an additional set of courses and community-based experiences to supplement their major programs of study.

| Pre-UC Program | Students typically apply to the program in spring semester of freshman year. Some students apply during their sophomore years, but we encourage students to apply as early as possible in order to benefit from the full program. |
|---|---|
| Empower I & II (1st year seminar) | Empower is a yearlong seminar that all UC students take during the first year in the program. The course helps students begin to interrogate power, privilege, and oppression and to understand the systemic nature of oppression. This course prompts students to interrogate their own identities and begin to understand the importance of service and social justice. UC students work with student mentors (ranging between 5th-10th grade) who engage in Youth Participatory Action Research (YPAR) projects, delving deeper into issues of concern to the student mentors. This process allows UC students to more deeply understand the assets and challenges of the urban context and the ways in which systemic oppression impacts the lives of youth. Furthermore, and most important to the UC, youth voice is valued and centered as they are recognized as agents of change. |
| Weekend Immersion | Students are required to take part in one weekend immersion experience. This takes place at the beginning of the program in Over-the-Rhine (OTR) in Cincinnati. Students spend 2 nights with their cohort in an urban community where they learn about the community's history, take a community tour, take part in educational activities to further their knowledge about the community, participate in community service, and reflect on their experiences. |
| Cincinnati Summer Immersion Program (CSIP) or Cleveland | CSIP & COSI immersions are 3-6 weeks long and take place in the summer or during winter break in Cincinnati and Cleveland. UC students are required to participate in at least one of the immersion experiences, and some students opt to participate in both. During the immersion, students live in an urban community or with a family who has volunteered to house them. Monday-Thursday, students are assigned to work in 1-2 service agencies in their host communities. Their hours and experiences in these agencies vary depending |

| | |
|---|---|
| Ohio Community Immersion (COSI) | upon the needs of the agency and community. Students also attend two classes on Fridays, one that prompts them to think about and discuss urban teaching and one that provides deeper understanding of urban communities, history, and systemic oppression. Students participate in weekly journaling sessions and give presentations at the end of their experience in a community space. |
| Junior Seminar (2nd year) | The junior seminar helps students further understand what it means to be an accomplished urban community practitioner (e.g. teacher, social worker, doctor, etc.) and provides students opportunities to connect theory and practice. Class is held twice a month at the university and once a month in Over-the-Rhine at the Peaslee Neighborhood Center. Campus seminars focus on issues of justice in urban communities and schools. Our community-based seminars occur in one of our partner agencies focusing on current community challenges and what it means to be an agent of change while working alongside the folks in the struggle. These seminars also prompt students to think deeply about the social and cultural issues students face in urban schools and to begin to develop educational and professional values that can be put into practice. During this phase of the program students work alongside a group of community mentors who co-teach the community-based seminars. |
| Senior Seminar (3rd year) | The senior seminar takes place during the semester when the students are not student teaching. In this seminar, they read texts pertaining to urban education, discuss issues faced during student teaching, and learn about classroom management from experienced, collaborating, in-service, urban teachers. |
| Student teaching (Optional Residency Program) & Student Teaching Seminar | The Residency Program is an option open to all UC students. Participating UC students are required to student teach in an urban school. Students take part in a student teaching seminar that is led by the UC faculty member who is the student teaching supervisor. They discuss issues that arise for the student teachers, such as: classroom management, family-community-school partnerships, pedagogy, and job search skills and requirements. Residency Program students live in the community for the entire semester, attend journaling sessions, and attend the American City course that is co-taught by a Miami faculty member and a long-time community member. Residency Program students complete a final presentation at the end of the semester at the Miami University Center for Community Engagement (AKA buddy's Place) located in Over-the-Rhine. |

**Peaslee Neighborhood Center**

Figure 2: Peaslee Center Mural

Figure 2: Peaslee Center Mural

The Peaslee Neighborhood Center, located in the historic neighborhood of Over-the-Rhine in Cincinnati, OH, is one of the UC's long-time community partners. The neighborhood is in the late stages of gentrification, and Peaslee Neighborhood is one of a handful of grassroots organizations that have firmly planted their feet in the ground of the quickly changing area and have refused to be pushed out to make way for high-rise condos or boutique hotels. Peaslee's mission statement shines a light on the important work that takes place within their walls:

> *Peaslee Neighborhood Center is a peaceful place in Over-The-Rhine where residents create and engage in participatory education to foster creative expression, self-determination, and social change.* (Peaslee Neighborhood Center, 2018, n.p.)

This powerful community asset has deep roots of resistance and has weathered its fair share of battles to remain in the community. Peaslee was formerly an Elementary school with the same name (Peaslee Elementary School). In 1982, the elementary school was closed, and two concerned mothers, Everlene Leary and Kathleen Prudence, started a campaign to keep the school open. The group of women who began organizing with the founding mothers called themselves the Peaslee Women's Working Committee. The committee did not end up saving the school, but they didn't give up. They decided to raise the funds to purchase the building in order to keep Peaslee as an important community asset. It's important to note that the committee included white and Black working-class women who didn't have access to large sums of money. Despite not having personal wealth, the women worked hard to raise the funds to purchase the building. On December 14, 1984, the group of women bought the building for $209, 239.13, ensuring that Peaslee could remain an important community hub. Peaslee has been going strong for 34 years because of the hard work and determination of the mothers who decided to take action to save Peaslee (Peaslee Neighborhood Center, 2018, n.p.).

The history of Peaslee provides insight and understanding into the strong sense of community, love, and resistance that is present in this sacred space that serves as the UC program's second home. Sharing these stories is important, because "telling stories is one of the ways that we can begin the process of building community" (hooks, 2010, p. 49). This is a story we want to raise up as a powerful example of what radical love looks like in action. Another community partner, housed in a space of love and resistance, is Miami University's Center for Community Engagement, also known as buddy's Place. This is where the optional Over-the-Rhine Residency Program takes place.

**Over-the-Rhine Residency Program**

Figure 3: Miami Center for Community Engagement Mural

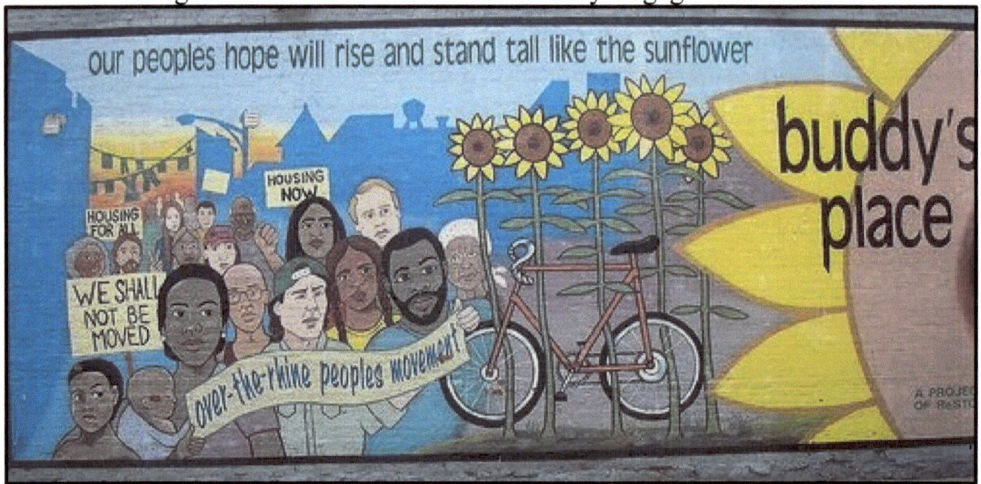

The Miami University Over-the-Rhine Residency Program was created in 2006 through a collaboration of members of the Over-the-Rhine community in Cincinnati and Tom Dutton, former Director of the Miami University Center for Community Engagement in Over-the-Rhine. As stated on the Center for Community Engagement (2010) website, "the Residency Program constitutes a particular model for community engagement that expands the opportunities of community service beyond programs based on charity, vanguardism, and noblesse oblige." This is a program designed to impact the hearts and minds of students and to expand their notions of what it means to live and work in an urban community.

Throughout their time in the residency program, students engage in service, as well as learn about the history, current social-cultural understandings, and power dynamics in the urban neighborhood where they are living, attending class, and working for the semester. The program seeks to change the social class affiliation of students in order to change and expand their class interests so that they see themselves as part of a larger social struggle to advocate for justice in urban communities (Dutton, 2014). This is a process, and students don't get there overnight, if at all, but that is one of the goals of the residency program. Students who are coming into a community that is not their own must be careful that they do not take on a savior mentality and that they learn to walk alongside community members. This is something that is emphasized within the residency program classes.

Students spend an entire semester living, working, and taking courses within the community of Over-the-Rhine. Students either live in the student residency house located in Over-the-Rhine or in an apartment near the residency house. The Architecture and Interior Design majors design and build projects in the community that benefit low-income residents (Center for Community Engagement in Over-the-Rhine, 2010), while students who are participating from other majors work in community-based organizations (e.g. the Worker's Center, Peaslee Neighborhood Center, Over-the-Rhine Community Housing), a total of 24-27 hours per week. Teacher education majors (typically part of the UC program) complete their student teaching at one of the UC partner schools located in various neighborhoods in close proximity to the residency program.

Residency students also take a class called, The American City Since 1940, which is co-taught by a Miami faculty member and Bonnie Neumeier, who is a long-time community member, educator, and activist. The class was designed by the former director, Tom Dutton, who lost his battle with pancreatic cancer in 2017. It is due to the dedication of folks like Tom and Bonnie that we have the ability to work in the community of Over-the-Rhine. Tom was a compassionate, justice centered freedom fighter who fought side by side with community members for a more just and equitable community that served the interests of all community members. Although Tom did not live in the community, he was a loved and respected community member who dedicated his life to this work. Tom's passing was a great loss, but we carry this work forward with love and hope in our hearts. We ensure that students know who he was and how he lives on through this work by engaging with his work through readings, videos, and conversations.

The class meetings take place at Miami's Center for Community Engagement, also known as buddy's Place. This building holds a special significance to the community and the Over-the-Rhine People's Movement. The building symbolizes struggle, solidarity, and hope.

buddy's Place is named after long-time community activist buddy gray [buddy gray preferred his name in lower-case letters], who was tragically killed in 1996. buddy was one of the founding members of many of the social service organizations that still exist in Cincinnati today (e.g. Drop Inn Center, Homeless Coalition). Located above the Center for Community Engagement are 20 units of affordable, supportive housing specifically for folks who have recently experienced homelessness. The building was built brick by brick through the work of volunteers and members of the Over-the Rhine People's Movement who have cared deeply about the community long before the new wave of development took place.

Residency students also participate in a weekly reflection facilitated by Bonnie Neumeier at the student residency house. This is a time for students to open up and discuss their experiences each week working and living in the community. At the end of the semester, all of the residency students must complete a final project and present their projects at an open house hosted at buddy's Place. Community members, community organizations, teachers, Miami University faculty and administrators, friends, and family are invited to the open house to watch and engage with the student presentations, which include reflections of their experiences throughout the semester. This is a powerful program that seeks to merge theory and practice for both the benefit of the students who participate in the program and the communities in which they work and learn alongside community members. This type of community-based education is an important component of the UC program and is being expanded to include local K-12 teachers in weekend teacher immersions. For teachers, this program provides a means to more fully understand the lived experiences of their students and the material realities they are facing. Residency programs take education outside of the traditional classroom walls in order to help students better understand the social, cultural, and material realities in urban communities.

**Description of Over-the-Rhine**

Over-the-Rhine is a small neighborhood located in Cincinnati's urban core and has been at the center of much debate over the last 18 years and a space of social struggle for even longer. It was put on the National Register of Historic Places in 1984, which put the impoverished neighborhood at greater risk for gentrification by the rich gentry who now seek to take back the valuable, contested land (Dutton, 2007). The narratives used to tell the history of Over-the-Rhine leave much of the rich history of social struggle completely out of the story. The current narrative suggests that Over-the-Rhine was once a dark, scary place where nothing was happening, where no one lived or wanted to live, but now Over-the-Rhine is going through an Urban Renaissance, and finally, there are dedicated people there who care about the community (Dutton, 2014). This essentially erases the story of the Over-the-Rhine People's Movement, which has a rich history of social struggle and collective solidarity forged to "build a way out of no way" (Personal Communication, Jennifer Summers, April 18, 2015).

The People's Movement has been present in the community since the late 1960s and continues to work to keep a place for working class and working poor folks in the community, a community that is quickly being reclaimed and rebranded by people with more access to capital. The People's Movement, a collective of concerned citizens that cuts across race, class, and gender differences is responsible for much of the affordable housing that is still in the community and many of the social services that are now slowly being pushed out of the community. The latest wave of gentrification began in 2003 when the city abolished the planning department and gave preferred development status to Cincinnati Center City Development Corporation (3CDC), a non-profit organization whose board consists of many of the corporate businesses in Cincinnati (Dutton, 2012). Essentially, corporate Cincinnati now unofficially runs the city's planning department and decides whose voices get included and excluded around development in OTR. This approach to city planning is antithetical to democracy and works to exclude the voices of the citizens who are most gravely impacted by the corporate agenda in Cincinnati (Skirtz, 2012).

Over-the-Rhine, similar to many urban neighborhoods across the nation, has experienced significant changes in recent years. Vine Street, the main thoroughfare in Over-the-Rhine, once deemed a dangerous, crime-filled drug haven, is now lined with expensive shops and restaurants and luxury condos that have taken the place of much of the affordable housing that once filled the neighborhood. The "Gateway Quarter," an area in the southwest corner of Over-the-Rhine has become a residential area for mostly white, young professionals and hipsters and a "sanitized urban playground for the privileged," which includes visitors from the suburbs (Dutton, 2012, p. 5).

Many folks in Cincinnati see the development in Over-the-Rhine as progress and applaud the gentrification that has come with the development of the neighborhood. They now consider the neighborhood "safe" for young, white people who want to spend their time and money in the trendy new scene. Dutton (2012) describes the sweeping gentrification taking place in Over-the-Rhine as "the mobilization of corporate and state power to purge undesirables—the excluded—from view, from democratic processes, from social life. Apparently, we used to exploit the poor; now we try to dispose of them" (p. 5). Although corporate Cincinnati and many of its citizens, perhaps fooled by the rhetoric of the media, merely see gentrification as a necessary part of urban development, scholars such as Diskin and Dutton (2006) do not conceptualize gentrification and development as the same thing. They would argue that development can be done in such a way so that everyone is included in the planning process. The current wave of development and those behind it continue to push forward with their plans and, through the process of gentrification, are pushing out many long-time community members and important community assets and resources. This is the primary context in which we are engaging in our work, and this information provides a deeper understanding of the social, cultural, and political struggles in which this work is located. We continue this work knowing that we may never get to the point where this struggle for liberation and justice is not necessary.

In his book, *Where Do We Go From Here: Chaos or Community?*, Martin Luther King, Jr. (1968) writes:

> *A vigorous enforcement of civil rights will bring an end to separate, public facilities, but it cannot bring an end to fears, prejudice, pride and irrationality, which are the barriers to a truly integrated society. These dark and demonic responses will be removed only as men are possessed by the invisible inner law which etches on their hearts the conviction that all men are brothers and that love is mankind's most potent weapon for personal and social transformation.* (pp. 106-107)

While we are a small cadre of folks working together across multiple spaces and identities for social transformation, and while we know we are merely making a dent, we do so with love, a radical orientation to love that is real and hard and risky and painful and forces us to look at our own "dark and demonic" ways of being in the world. We do so in order that we all may become better humans working for a more just society.

# References

Center for Community Engagement in Over-the-Rhine. (2010). *Residency program.* Retrieved from https://blogs.miamioh.edu/cce-otr/residency-program

Diskin, J., & Dutton, T. (2006). *Gentrification—It ain't what you think.* https://blogs.miamioh.edu/cce-otr/files/2016/10/Gentrification-It-Aint-What-You-Think.pdf

Dutton, T. A. (2007). Colony Over-the-Rhine. *The Black Scholar, 37*(3), 14-27.

Dutton, T. A. (2012). *Do you have a sign?* Retrieved from https://blogs.miamioh.edu/cce-otr/files/2016/10/Do-You-Have-a-Sign.pdf

Dutton, T. A. (2014). *Econocide Over-the-Rhine.* Retrieved from https://blogs.miamioh.edu/cce-otr/files/2016/10/Econocide-Over-the-Rhine.pdf

Flynn, J. E., Rolon-Dow, R., & Worden, L. J. (2018). The responsibilities of white teacher candidates and teacher educators in developing racial literacy. *Multicultural Perspectives, 20*(4), 240-246.

hooks, b. (2003). *Teaching community: A pedagogy of hope.* New York, NY: Routledge.

hooks, b. (2010). *Teaching critical thinking: Practical wisdom.* New York, NY: Routledge.

King, M. L., Jr. (1968). *Where do we go from here: Chaos or community?* Boston, MA: Beacon Press.

Klein, E., Taylor, M., Onore, C., Strom, K., & Abrams, L. (2013). Finding a third space in teacher education: Creating an urban teacher residency. *Teaching Education, 24*(1), 27-57.

Ladson-Billings, G. (2017). "Makes me wanna holler": Refuting the "culture of poverty" discourse in urban schooling. *The Annals of the American Academy of Political and Social Science, 673*(1), 80-90.

Longo, N. (2007). *Why community matters: Connecting education with civic life.* New York, NY: State University of New York Press.

Murrell, P. C., Jr. (2001). *Community teacher: A new framework for effective urban teaching.* New York, NY: Teachers College Press.

Peaslee Neighborhood Center (PNC). (2018). *About us.* Retrieved from http://peasleecenter.org/about/

Sato, M., & Lensmire, T. J. (2009). Poverty and Payne: Supporting teachers to work with children of poverty. *Phi Delta Kappan, 90,* 365-370.

Skirtz, A. (2012). *Econocide: Elimination of the urban poor.* Washington, DC: NASW Press.

# Chapter 2: Using Youth Participatory Action Research to Combat Bullying

By Nick Sabet, Madison Allen, Natalie Zanardelli, Gaby Tagliamonte, Ashley Tackett

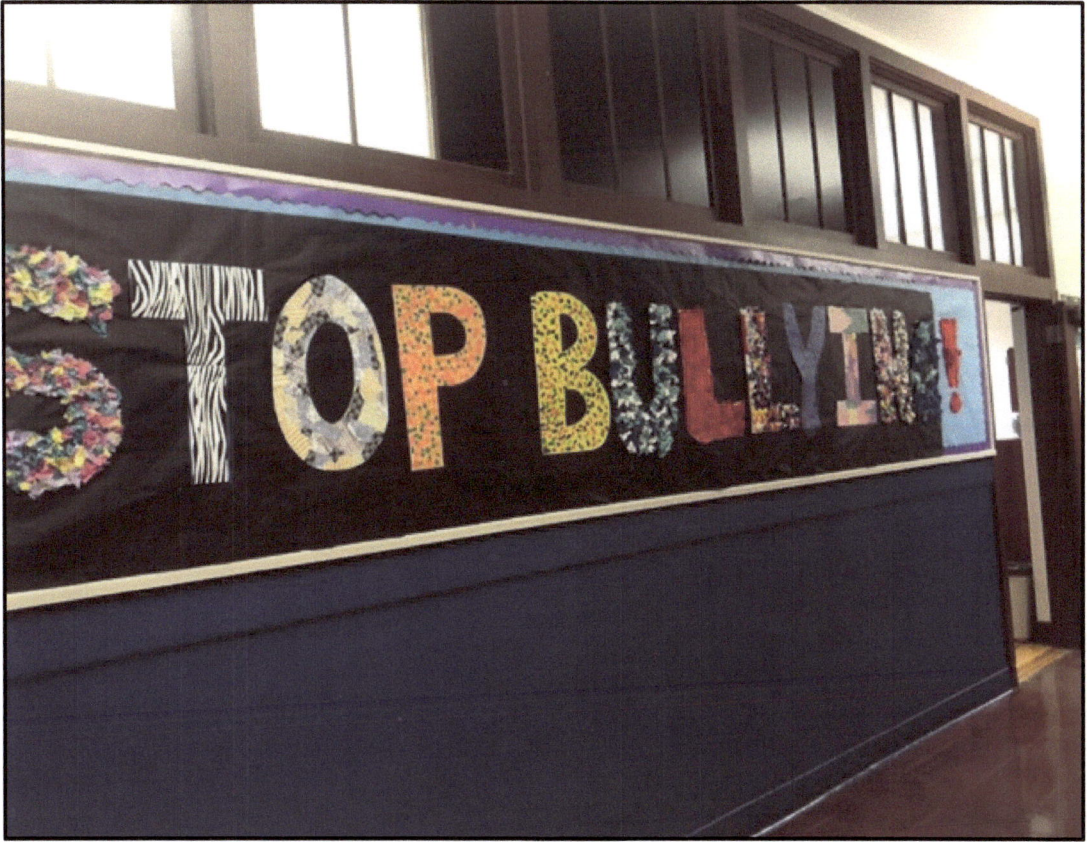

During the 2016-2017 school year, the Urban Cohort worked alongside youth mentors at Urban STEM School in Cincinnati, Ohio, on the issue of bullying in their school. The students identified bullying as a huge problem in their school, and they wanted to take action. Through Youth Participatory Action Research (YPAR), which included hours of research and surveys, we made progress and saw changes in their school. In this chapter, we will discuss the collective process of addressing bullying at Urban STEM School.

Bullying is a widespread problem that impacts youth across the nation. According to a study conducted by Lessne and Yanez (2016), 20.8% of students reported being bullied, which is more than one out of every five students. While there isn't an agreed upon definition in the scholarly literature on bullying (Boyd, 2014), a common thread is that it is framed at the individual level. Bullying is often broadly defined as—interactions between an aggressor and a victim in which feelings are hurt—this simplistic definition can lead to overgeneralizations and a focus on the individual, as opposed to taking a look at how the system as a whole creates conditions that lead to and reinforce bullying. Pascoe (2014) suggests that bullying should be defined at the systemic level, as opposed to the individual level. She defines bullying as:

> *An interactional reproduction of structural inequalities that socializes young people into accepting social inequality. That is, the interactional process of bullying both builds on existing embodied, classed, raced, gendered and sexualized social inequalities and simultaneously prepares young people to accept such inequalities as a "normal" part of living in the world.* (para. 3)

Therefore, youth who engage in bullying behaviors are part of a larger system of social reproduction that is working to keep the status quo intact, a system that condemns difference and awards those who police difference. Youth who bully are not deviant. In fact, according to Pascoe (2014), "The young people are reinforcing said norms, acting, in effect, as agents of social reproduction of inequality—socializing others into accepting inequality" (para. 7). In order to effectively address bullying, it is imperative that we get to the root of the problem. Individual "bad" people are not the problem. Instead, a system is in place that perpetuates inequality and, thus, conditions young people to participate in a struggle for power and privilege. As powerfully stated by Sonya Renee Taylor (2018) in her book titled, *The Body is Not an Apology: The Power of Radical Self Love*, "the power to create laws also endows governments to influence, which bodies we accept as 'normal' and which we do not, all through the validation of legality" (p. 46). She points to the notion that body shame and the ways in which we police our bodies and the bodies of others on the basis of race, class, gender, sexuality, ability, etc. is directly tied to our legal and economic systems. Keeping people feeling shameful and shaming the bodies of others keeps the general population docile and pushes them to participate in the "Body Shame Profit Complex (BSPC)" that sells us overpriced products to tame our unruly bodies (p. 39).

Unfortunately, this system is already stacked against many youths based on their social locations. Yet, we can destabilize this system by conceptualizing youth as critically minded actors who can disrupt the status quo instead of merely accepting the current reality. YPAR provides a mode of resistance for young people engaged in the struggle for freedom and liberation. It is a space to collectively craft and engage with the power of radical self-love as proposed by Taylor (2018). In this chapter, we discuss the work that took place within our YPAR group.

Our YPAR group consisted of six college students and seven youth from our partner school. The group of youth were made up of six 6th graders and one 5th grader. To begin the YPAR process, the first thing we did as a group was sit down and discuss the issues that students saw within their community. The issue that came up the most was violence, and we eventually narrowed that down to bullying. We discussed the idea that violence in the community could be related to bullying, and the students thought that it was possible that kids were recreating behaviors that they saw in their communities or even their homes. If they see these behaviors and they become normalized, it is much more likely that they will replicate this behavior at school with their peers. In addition, these behaviors are part of a larger social system that perpetuates inequality. Thus, youth are often engaging in practices that reinforce their current social locations. Oppression takes on many forms, "bodies are not the only designators of oppression, but all oppression is enacted on the body" (Taylor, 2018, p. 81) Our students thought that bullying was a serious problem at their school, and they wanted to take the next steps to get to the bottom of it and take action.

The students decided to name themselves Urban STEM School For Action (USSFA), and their collective definition of bullying was "intentionally hurting someone physically or mentally using words or force." At this point in the process, the youth were still conceptualizing bullying at the individual level. Using their collective definition, they decided to send out a survey to grades 4-6 in their school. A major motivating factor for our research was the lack of available, critical, and multifaceted research on bullying of elementary school students. Much of the research that we found focused on individual types of bullying without narrowing down grade-level or other demographics, so we wanted to take a step forward and broaden the scope of bullying research among predominantly African-American elementary school students. The core component of our research was a survey that we created with the students at Urban STEM School. One hundred and fifty-six students took the survey. Presented below are the survey questions and results. It is important to note that the success of the survey required the buy-in of the other teachers and the principal. This speaks to the importance of building relationships with stakeholders outside of the core research group while conducting a YPAR project.

The specific results explicitly interpreted in this section of the chapter are the findings that the Urban STEM School group determined were most vital to the purpose of our research— collecting meaningful data about an under-researched issue in schools in order to contribute to the potential solutions that the students in Urban STEM School might devise. The results that are interpreted serve to further ground our dedication to the work and bring us closer to conclusions about bullying within Urban STEM School. While this is a short-term stepping stone within a massive plethora of objectives to be achieved by the other YPAR projects and despite technical differences in subject matter, all serve the same purpose of normalizing love and justice. As powerfully stated by Kelley (2002), "we need the strength to love and to dream" (p. xi). YPAR provides space for youth to engage in radical alternatives to the ways in which society currently operates. Perhaps, this is the first step on the path to liberation.

The survey consisted of 15 questions regarding the type of bullying experienced or witnessed by students, the number of times the student may have been bullied or bullied others, what grade level the bully is in, and if a teacher or parents had been told about bullying incidents. The list of questions and some of the possible responses are listed below.

| | |
|---|---|
| *1)* | *Have you ever been bullied?* |
| *2)* | *What type of bullying?*<br>   *a)  Mental*<br>   *b)  Physical*<br>   *c)  Cyber*<br>   *d)  Other* |
| *3)* | *If you have been bullied, where at?*<br>   *a)  Lunch*<br>   *b)  Recess*<br>   *c)  Specials\**<br>   *d)  Bus*<br>   *e)  Somewhere else in school*<br>   *f)  Other*<br>*\*"Specials" refers to the students' elective courses that change week by week, such as gym, music, art, etc.* |
| *4)* | *Is this the same person?* |
| *5)* | *How many times have you been bullied at school?* |
| *6)* | *How did you react to your bullying?* |
| *7)* | *Have you seen people being bullied?* |
| *8)* | *Do you feel comfortable going to an adult in the school about bullying?* |
| *9)* | *What grade did the bullying start?* |
| *10)* | *What grade level is your bully in?* |
| *11)* | *Have you told anyone that you've been bullied?* |
| *12)* | *Have you been bullied by more than one person?* |
| *13)* | *Have you ever bullied a person?* |
| *14)* | *If you have been a bully, how did you stop?* |
| *15)* | *How has this bullying affected your ability to learn?* |

Figure 1

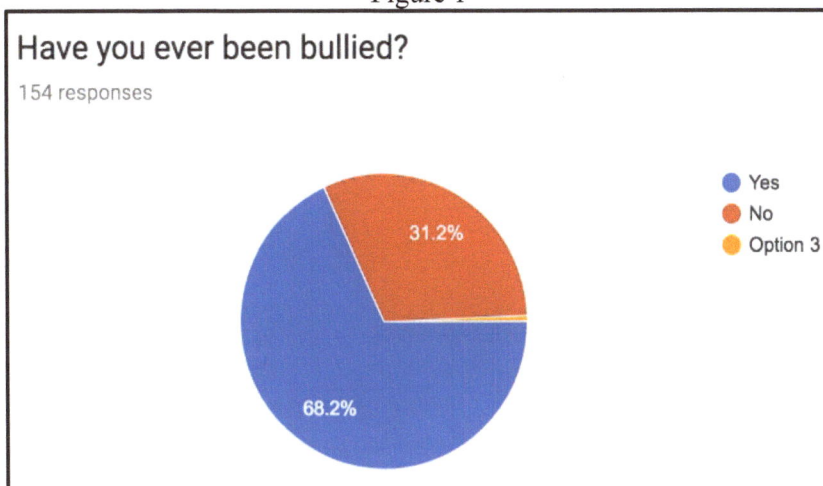

In response to the question, "Have you ever been bullied?" 68.2% of the respondents answered "yes," and 31.2% answered "no." The results to this question show that over half of the students who took the survey have been bullied. This noting of the result may not seem significant until one delves into the results of the question that followed. That question inquired about the types of bullying that the students have experienced. Of the respondents who answered that second question, 38.7% claimed to have experienced mental bullying, 24% claimed to have experienced physical bullying, 5.3% claimed to have experienced cyberbullying, and 32% selected that they had experienced a type or multiple types of bullying that weren't listed. It is crucial to draw attention to the result that mental bullying is the type of bullying that most of the respondents have experienced. People have traditionally thought of bullying as physical harm being inflicted upon an individual by another individual. Students may experience multiple types of bullying, but the fact that mental bullying was the largest response leads us to assert that bullying has taken on new forms and has been refined and redefined through the years.

Mental bullying can be considered an umbrella term over verbal bullying, among other types of non-physical bullying. Proving that these types of bullying events have occurred can be difficult, hence their growth in prevalence among students. With countless anti-bullying policies being implemented in schools across the country (U.S. Department of Health and Human Services, 2018), one can assume that bullies have taken more underground approaches to committing their crime. If this survey were given to high school students, it is reasonable to assume that cyber bullying or mental bullying would be the majority of the result, as there has been a rise in cyberbullying due to increased access to technology and internet platforms (Dennehy, Cronin, & Arensman, 2019). Cyberbullying is identified as "an international public health concern" and is more closely correlated with depression and thoughts of suicide than traditional forms of bullying (Dennehy, Cronin, & Arensman, 2019, p. 54). The nuance of this result in elementary schools arises from the fact that not all of the students in this particular school may have access to technology for purposes of constant communication with their peers.

In addition, the students responded that 43.1% were bullied by the same person and 39.6% were bullied by a different person. Since most of the students who answered are targeted by the same individual, it would be valuable to ask what makes certain individuals target others. We could inquire what exactly students in Urban STEM School are targeted for (e.g. size, physical disability, mental disabilities, race, family history, social class). If we discover what encourages repeat offenses of harm by bullies against their targets, we can understand where to focus reform in the effort of creating accepting spaces for students. For example, we might question whether we focus more heavily on educating students about how making fun of someone's size hurts the target, rather than how students with mental disabilities are targeted. No student's issue is more important than another's when it comes to curbing bullying, but it is worth examining the reasons that people are bullied and whether or not those reasons are integrated in a larger trend of what causes students to be targeted.

In one alarming response to a survey question, 77.3% of the students responded that they have witnessed bullying. Over three-fourths of the students have witnessed someone else being bullied. One follow-up question we should have asked is whether or not they did anything when they saw the bullying taking place, such as telling the bully to stop or reporting it to a teacher or another adult. One beneficial outcome of the survey was that we learned that most students are comfortable telling an adult about bullying (see *Figure 2*).

Figure 2

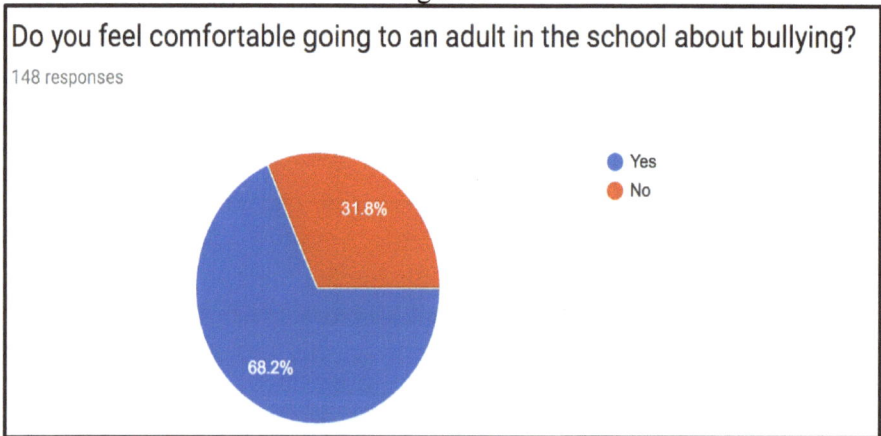

Do you feel comfortable going to an adult in the school about bullying?
148 responses

Yes
No

31.8%

68.2%

The students say they are comfortable going to an adult to talk about bullying. According to question 11, "Have you told anyone that you've been bullied," 63.3% of the students have told someone that they've been bullied. However, reporting bullying does not seem to have improved the bullying situation at Urban STEM School, since the survey also showed that almost 75% of students have been bullied. The results show that most students (60.4%) are only bullied by one individual, but the next question that asked if the students have ever bullied a person garnered interesting results, as shown in *Figure 3*.

Figure 3

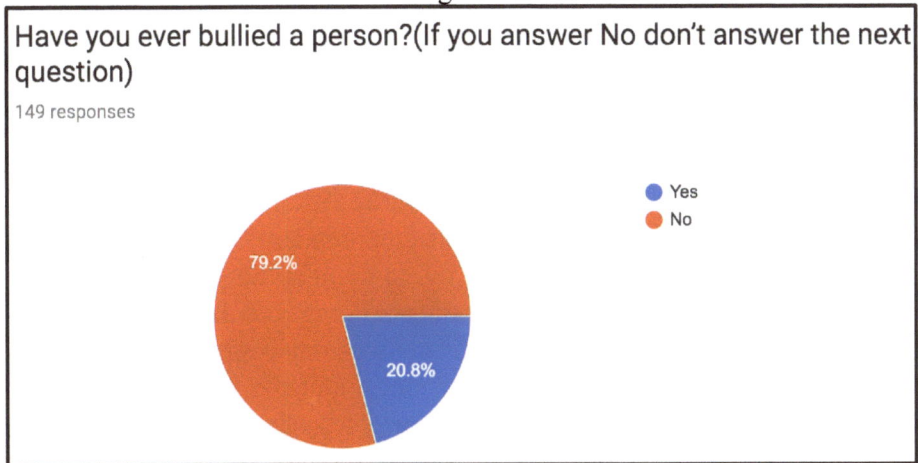

Have you ever bullied a person?(If you answer No don't answer the next question)

149 responses

- Yes
- No

79.2%

20.8%

Only 20.8% of the students admitted to bullying another person. Even though the survey was anonymous, students may not want to admit that they have bullied someone, or students may not realize their behaviors are consistent with bullying, so these results are perhaps skewed. It would be interesting to conduct focus groups to dig a little deeper into these issues.

**Taking a Collective Stand Against Bullying**

The USSFA students and their teacher were very surprised with the results of the survey. They had an idea that bullying was happening within their school, but they didn't realize it was such a widespread issue. It really solidified for everyone that this was the issue that we not only *wanted* to address as a collective but *needed* to address.

From there, we brainstormed ways to take action to make a change within the school. While we knew that change takes time and we would not be able to see huge results right away, we also knew that small changes may lead to gradual, lasting change. The first thing the students wanted to do was create a bullying box, which would sit in the office and be a place where kids could put notes about bullying incidents that they had witnessed or experienced. The notes could be anonymous or not. The purpose of the box was mainly so that teachers could be informed of bullying taking place, while also taking the pressure off of the students to tell them in person. An idea for an app, perhaps a future project, stemmed off of the box idea, so if students had smartphones, they could report cases of bullying even more quickly.

Another thing that the kids wanted to do was make April Anti-Bullying Month at their school. To do this, we spent time making colorful, creative posters that they would hang up around their school to raise awareness. They also applied for a grant to fund buying items with anti-bullying messages on them for the students at Urban STEM School. Some of the items were pencils, lanyards, rubber bracelets, and t-shirts designed with anti-bullying slogans. The students decided that they wanted to create a website to promote Anti-Bullying Month and other anti-bullying events around the school. We worked closely with the students to create the website they envisioned, and it was launched soon after.

Perhaps the two biggest things that the students put together during the YPAR work was a PowerPoint that they presented at a parent/teacher/student anti-bullying night at their school and a play about bullying. The anti-bullying night at the school went very well, and it got positive feedback from parents and students. Over 100 families attended the anti-bullying night, and there were even students from other schools in attendance. A post-event survey was administered to students at the school about the impact of the anti-bullying event, and 100% of the respondents said they learned something new and felt the event was beneficial. In addition, the students worked hard to make the play something that would be impactful and informative, while also entertaining. They wrote everything themselves and practiced it so that they were able to perform it for everyone involved in the Urban Cohort at the end of the year and eventually in a school performance. It was a big hit.

Bullying is not an issue that has one simple answer. It is unique to every school, so every school has to take a different approach to addressing the problem. The steps that we took at Urban STEM School to address bullying will not immediately make everything better. However, the fact that we are taking initiative and making small strides to tackle bullying will hopefully lead to a chain reaction within the student body and faculty at Urban STEM School. More importantly, youth who are engaged in the YPAR process may begin to see themselves as capable leaders and citizens who can bring change to their communities. As stated by Torre and Fine (2006) "participation lies at the core of democracy and justice" (p. 269). The YPAR process is much more important than the end results of the actions. The process puts youth on a path, and the hope is that the path will continue long after the project has ended.

## Impact on Youth Mentors

One of the most inspiring parts of our YPAR work came from a writing exercise we asked the mentors to do. We asked each mentor to demonstrate what they had gotten from the YPAR work in any form they wished (e.g. poem, picture, etc.). We received both poems and pictures. The poems were inspiring, as the mentors detailed how their own perceptions of bullying and their school environment had changed. They described the consequences of bullying—both for the bully and the one being bullied—and shared how this new knowledge affected them. One poem expressed what being a bully means, saying things like "having an ugly attitude" and "telling lies." This mentor also wrote about what she believed to be one of the causes of bullying. She wrote, "Bullies have nasty, horrible feelings and could be hurting other people because they are getting hurt in a bad way." The intriguing aspect of the poems is the reader's ability to see the journey of each mentor as they began to comprehend the complexity of bullying and why it is so prevalent in our schools today.

> *When you bully it's not very kind*
> *Please stop the bullying, keep it in mind*
> *Don't bully just because you've been bullied before*
> *All the anger you have to store*
> *Storing all your anger isn't going to help*
> *When people get bullied they don't always scream for help*
> *Try hard not to bully at any time*
> *Just keep this in mind*
> *Bullying people leads to sadness or death*
> *Don't be mean and take away people's breath*
> *When you bully it's not very kind*
> *Please stop the bullying, keep it in mind*

The student who wrote this poem also expressed how the program has helped her: "This leadership program has benefited me because I am very open now, and I have made new friends. I have worked harder than ever before."

The pictures, similar to the poems, also tell the story of each mentor as they began to delve deeper into bullying in all of its forms. The first picture illustrated a girl with a tear trickling down her face as hurtful words float around her. These words include "stupid," "fat," "annoying," and "overly-dramatic." When asked about what inspired the mentor to include these specific words, she explained that these are words she has heard in her own school many times before. The inspiration for the crying girl came from her school too, as she explained that many of the girls are seen crying on a daily basis because of bullying. Another picture captured a similar theme as the one before but with a positive spin. The second picture portrayed the outline of a body with words of encouragement enveloping it. Phrases such as "be kind," "love all," and "heart and mind unite" adorned the page with decorative doodles. When asked about her picture, this mentor said that she took a more positive approach with the hopes of giving courage to those who read it.

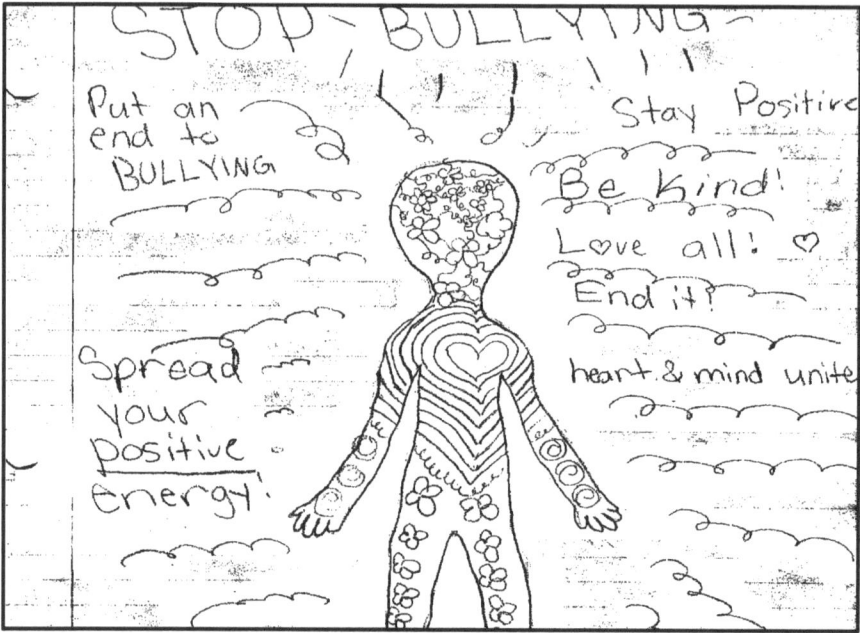

Comparing the first two pictures was incredible, as we could see how the two mentors interpreted and were affected by our collective work in their own ways. The final picture related greatly to the first picture. In this depiction, a chart was created linking bullying to its various consequences—suicide, depression, fear, etc. From the consequences, a line was drawn connecting each one to a phrase one might use when experiencing those consequences. When asked about the chart, this mentor said that the goal was to educate people about the effects of bullying, as well as provide helpful indicators and phrases to determine if someone has been bullied.

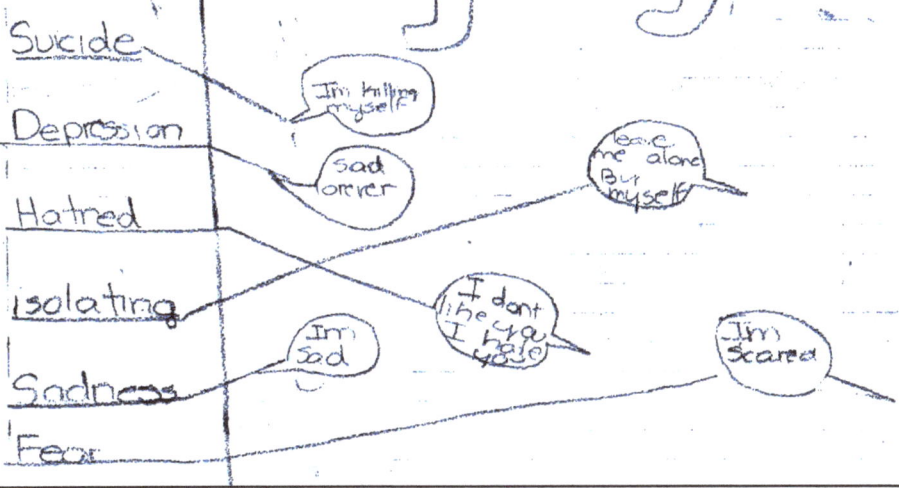

> This program has helped me alot. At first I thought I knew the definition of bullying but I didn't. This program has brought my understanding to a whole new level. It let me know im making a difference at school. Also how many students lives it will change. I was introduced some new people. This is a amazing program. Im helping to make a difference in life
>
> **Bullying**
> Suicide — "Im killing myself"
> Depression — "Sad forever"
> Hatred — "leave me alone Buy myself"
> Isolating — "I dont like me I hate you"
> Sadness — "Im Sad"
> Fear — "Im Scared"

We asked the mentors many times before to talk about how they felt in regard to bullying and the work we had done. However, nothing had ever spoken as much as their creative writing and artwork. Allowing the mentors to take a more creative interpretation of their feelings showed us just how impactful our time together had been. The messages within their writing and artwork portrayed more than what the mentors had ever expressed to us before. Having a creative outlet gave them the ability to express the things that words could not.

Furthermore, after prompting the mentors to express their feelings about our work, we then asked them to write a short paragraph about the things they had learned and how they felt the work has impacted themselves, as well as their school. The answers were fairly similar, most of which concluded that the work had greatly improved the bullying epidemic in their school. The paragraphs shared the same themes as the creative writing/drawings—that bullying has taken on a new meaning for them and that they want to spread their knowledge to their friends and peers in order to work towards the eradication of bullying in their school and beyond.

## Impact on Miami Students

The YPAR experience impacted  our views about our future role as educators and our views about the work that will come with that career path. Our resolve to be educators has been heightened by this experience of working with the student mentors. Although we, as future teachers, may be thought to be cogs in a machine that has formally engineered us to manufacture and sell passive minds to the world, we have come to the conclusion that we do not want that to be our destiny, nor do we want it to be our students' destinies. We, instead, desire to sow conscious, curious, and just minds into the winds of the world. The YPAR experience reaffirmed our commitment to sending critical thinkers and changemakers into the world. As educators we believe this is the essential core of our objective in the timeless and often thankless work of this justice-seeking business, and it now holds a nuanced place in our hearts and in our minds. This nuance is characterized by what the mentors brought to the table in the mission of justice.

We expected to take the role of main researchers, telling the youth mentors about what we did and then letting them present the data to express what "they" had discovered. Instead, we found ourselves taking a role of guidance and facilitation. The students created their own questions for their research and executed their duties in these efforts. A point came in the research when we felt that, if we were not learning with the students about our topic, then at least we were learning from them. There was no reason to dwell on the lulls in which discourse was lacking and in which tasks were being completed at a slower pace than one would prefer because the students always found their way back to the passion and to the state of acknowledging why they participated in this work in the first place. We now see that youth are cognizant of the issues around them, and we see that they are willing to put in the work to make change if they are given the opportunity. We are encouraged and excited by this fact as we work towards the dawn of our teaching careers.

## Conclusion

Although we did not resolve bullying in its totality, we did start the process. With our mentors, we were able to plant a seed that will grow in our mentors' schools and communities and everywhere they go in life. By having these educated and emancipatory conversations with the youth, we have co-created the knowledge and confidence needed to battle bullying in any form they see it. This also has the potential to extend to other issues of injustice that they come up against in the various contexts in which they find themselves. As Freire (1970) stated, "a deepened consciousness of their situation leads people to apprehend that situation as an historical reality susceptible of transformation" (p. 85). Understanding that there is hope in the struggle for liberation is a very important lesson that we all learned through this process. The mentors have expressed that their school is a different place—imagine what the world would look like if every student felt compelled to seek and capable of creating social change within their communities and schools. The world can be reimagined and remade. We only have to dare to dream and inspire others to dream with us and reimagine a society with a foundation of love and justice.

# References

Boyd, D. (2014). *It's complicated: The social lives of networked teens.* New Haven, CT: Yale University Press.

Dennehy, R., Cronin, M., & Arensman, E. (2019). Involving young people in cyberbullying research: The implementation and evaluation of a rights-based approach. *Health Expectations, 22*(1), 54-64.

Freire, P. (1970). *Pedagogy of the oppressed.* New York, NY: Continuum.

Lessne, D., & Yanez, C. (2016). *Student reports of bullying: Results from the 2015 school crime supplement to the national crime victimization survey.* Washington DC: National Center for Education Statistics. Retrieved from https://nces.ed.gov/pubsearch/pubsinfo.asp?pubid=2017015

Pascoe, C. J. (2014). Bullying as social inequality. *The Enemy, 1*(1). Retrieved from http://theenemyreader.org/wp-content/uploads/2014/02/Pascoe_The_Enemy.pdf

Taylor, S. R. (2018). *The Body is not an apology: The power of radical self-love.* Oakland, CA: Berrett-Koehler Publishers, Inc.

Torre, M., & Fine, M. (2006). Researching and resisting: Democratic policy research by and for youth. In S. Ginwright, P. Noguera, & J. Cammarota (Eds.), *Beyond resistance! Youth activism and community change. New democratic possibilities for practice and policy for America's youth* (pp. 269-285). New York, NY: Routledge.

U.S. Department of Health and Human Services. (2018). *Laws, policies & regulations.* Retrieved from https://www.stopbullying.gov/laws/index.html

# Interlude

## YPAR Project Introduction: MLK High School

By Andrea Spenny, teacher

I am a graduate of Miami University and the Urban Cohort program. I am now an English teacher in a local, urban high school. I primarily work with 9th and 10th graders and joined the Youth Participatory Action Research (YPAR) team because I feel this approach to curriculum, pedagogy, and leadership development is useful in my classroom and for my students. My students are often deemed as "less-than" by certain members of society because of their skin color, their age, their socioeconomic status, or the school they attend. My students are often deemed as "less-than" because of their culture. My students are often deemed as "less-than" when they attempt to use their voices to challenge, to question, or to help fight for positive change. Due to this, many members of society often silence them. Through YPAR, students learn that their voices are valued and that they should not be silenced. By the time they meet me in 10th grade, many believe that they do not have a voice or that their voice does not matter or that they are not allowed to use their voice. Or, they subconsciously choose not to use their voice because of the ways in which various social systems have raised them. One of these systems is school.

Schools love to proclaim how they "prepare students for the real world," which implies that our students are not currently living in the real world, and therefore, they are not a part of the real world until they graduate from high school. This is problematic. Schools may not realize this implication. Or, possibly, schools do realize this implication and choose not to care about the message they our sending our kids—that students current lives are not valued as a part of the "real world," that they do not experience any of the issues or challenges they will experience in the "real world," and that they must graduate high school to enter the "real world."

This message leaves me disheartened and terrified. This message dismisses the cultural experiences of my students. This message leaves out my students who may not earn a high school diploma when they are "supposed to" for one reason or another. This message tells my students that their lived experiences hold no value. This message dehumanizes my students.

One method of resisting these messages is using the power that I hold as a classroom teacher to use YPAR to supplement our district-created curriculum. YPAR is one small, but very impactful, way for my kids to realize they DO matter, that they ARE living in the real world, and that they CAN use their voices. YPAR has allowed my students to express themselves in ways that they've never been given the opportunity or been allowed to before. However, neither YPAR, nor I, nor any one individual or program can fix what the system has done to some of our children.

I had 5 students who worked with YPAR in one way or another throughout the school year. Though my students focused on school discipline and policies, some of them still continue to find themselves in situations in which they are receiving discipline due to fighting, skipping class, etc. Some of these kids are still failing multiple classes. Some people may have the attitude of, "See? Why do you even give them this opportunity or try to help? They're always going to be the same." The system has done a lot of harm and caused significant trauma from the time these students first entered school until now, when they are 16 or 17 years old. That trauma and hurt and pain cannot be eradicated within one year or because of one program. These kids, just like all of us, are on their own journeys and have their own stories. I do not condone some of my students' actions or choices in regard to their interactions with school, but I firmly believe we must look at what parts of the system may be to blame for some of their actions or choices.

My students chose to focus on school-wide and district-wide discipline policies, as they believe many of them are ineffective. Our school has one of the highest disciplinary occurrence rates in the entire district. Many students in our school experience trauma outside of school, which plays into some of the discipline occurrences within our building. The YPAR students chose to develop a survey to gather student feedback on certain discipline policies in hopes to use this data to make a change. Though my YPAR group had large dreams and goals for this project, we realized quickly that acting on the gathered data would take much more time. However, by the end of the school year, my students did feel empowered through their YPAR experience. Even though they did not fully accomplish what they had hoped to accomplish, they were able to learn the process behind what it takes to make a positive change and know that they can put that process to use in their future.

# Chapter 3:

# Youth Push Back on the Disciplining of "Unruly" Bodies in the Classroom

By James Hodges, Rachel Hollins, Emily Eaton, Liyanna Chandler-Nieves, Bridget LaRock

According to resistance theory, youth have always "understood in deep, complex, contradictory and embodied ways, the very systems which were oppressing them" (Fine, Tuck, & Yang, 2014, p. 46). Yet, youth are often positioned as incapable of understanding the complex realities of systemic oppression or the role that social politics plays in shaping our public policy. Despite the power and capability of youth of color and youth who live in urban communities, their voices are often silenced in conversations about public policy. They are not viewed as valuable members of society who have the potential to be agents of social change (Mirra, Garcia, & Morrell, 2016). Furthermore, even in schools across the nation that are supposedly geared towards the pursuit of knowledge and higher thinking, youth are often not challenged to critically analyze the world around them (Irizarry, 2009). Therefore, youth are not given the space to think introspectively about themselves, their social environments, and their role in society, thus, making them more susceptible to the cycle of systemic oppression in the United States and its various manifestations, including the school-to-prison pipeline and mass incarceration (Nocella, Parmar, & Stovall, 2014). The students are taught to read the word, but not the world (Freire & Macedo, 1987). However, a critical approach to education, tapping into their critical sensibilities, could lead to much different outcomes. As stated by Freire (1970), "a deepened consciousness of their situation leads people to apprehend that situation as a historical reality susceptible of transformation" (p. 85). Critical consciousness raising, or what Freire (1970) referred to as "conscientização," is a process that has the potential to transform the experiences of youth in urban schools and communities (p. 67).

Thus, when working with urban youth to support a heightened critical consciousness, a unique and critical approach to education is needed. This approach must counter the mundane, prison-like obedience, cookie-cutter style of our current education system, while also giving youth the opportunity to develop leadership skills. This is where Youth Participatory Action Research (YPAR) comes into play. YPAR is a research method that allows youth to become and act as experts on the issues impacting their communities and schools (Cammarota & Fine, 2008). Youth work alongside their peers, teachers, and community members to create positive change. As the experts, they conduct research and take action to eradicate, educate, and shed light on manifestations of oppression in their communities (Scott, Pyne, & Means, 2015). The YPAR process includes: (1) a collective approach, which requires community and relationship building; (2) a centering of the knowledge of youth; (3) an understanding of how race and other intersecting identities influence student experiences; (4) efforts to seek critical knowledge through research and consciousness raising; and (5) project implementation (action) and reflection (Cammarota & Fine, 2008). This is a powerful approach to both research and classroom curriculum and stands in stark contrast to the testing focused curriculum we see in many classrooms.

One of the most vital components of YPAR is the dialogue and relationship-building that takes place between the youth and the people looking to serve and immerse themselves in a community (in our case, the Miami University mentees). In traditional modes of research, researchers tend to treat people as numbers or objects to be observed and interpreted, instead of understanding them as humans with stories and history (Burke, Greene, & McKenna, 2017). Though they follow the scientific method, they often fail to capture meaningful results, because they miss the opportunity to create connections with the people they are researching. In addition, researchers often take their newfound "knowledge" outside of the community from which it originated (Mirra et al., 2016). This approach undermines people, compromising their humanity by negating the personal histories that play a significant role in their lives. As such, it is antithetical to the community-based research approach YPAR takes up. YPAR's use of meaningful dialogue and community building as the means for collecting and sharing information is particularly important for two main reasons. First, it privileges the voices of youth and builds on their lived experiences and knowledge in order to further understand complex social issues (Grace & Langhout, 2014; Irizarry & Brown, 2014). Second, it helps students develop the critical consciousness that is necessary to reflect on their social environments and investigate their roles in society (Kohfeldt, Bowen, & Langhout, 2016). When adult mentees (i.e. Miami University Urban Cohort students) take the time to sit down, have conversations with their youth mentors, and ask thought-provoking questions, youth are shown not only that their voices matter and that adults care about what they have to say, but that they have the power to understand how institutional inequalities impact them. It is easy to believe and to perpetuate the narrative that youth are apathetic, but when given the chance to speak, youth are apt to develop nuanced opinions and ideas about issues that impact their communities and schools. During our time with our youth mentors from MLK High School (MLKHS), we learned quickly how important the power of dialogue and community building was to our ability to meet our YPAR goals.

Before we go into further detail about our time at MLKHS, it is important for us to include a statement about our own positionalities. Two of the Miami students identify as white, upper middle class, females. Two of the Miami students previously attended Cincinnati Public Schools (CPS), identify as African American, are of low socioeconomic status, and therefore, have a deeper understanding of the community and school context. The six students with whom we worked were Black, 14-16 years old, and many had experienced living in poverty. The demographics of the students we worked with aligns with the school-wide demographics at MLKHS. At MLKHS over 90% of the students identify as Black,

Non-Hispanic, and over 95% are identified as being economically disadvantaged. The graduation rate at MLKHS is 60%. Many argue that these statistics come with a negative connotation and, therefore, feel that they can label and judge MLKHS in whatever ways they wish. The students and their teacher don't stand for that. Their teacher firmly believes that the demographics of their school are a source of strength and a constant encouragement to do better.

Despite the strengths of the school, MLKHS faces many unique challenges, and some of the public, as well as some of the students, view this school as needing a more positive culture, particularly when it comes to school discipline. It's important to point out that many of the students at the school, including some of the students we worked with on the project, believed that the "problem" existed in the behaviors of individual students and not the systemic structures that are in place both in and outside of the school that impact the lives of youth and their families. Many of the youth we worked with discussed facing unfair discipline policies, contributing to the phenomenon known as the school-to-prison pipeline. The school-to-prison pipeline is a national problem, stemming from the same policies that impact adults within the criminal justice system. Skiba, Arrendondo, and Williams (2014) define the school-to-prison pipeline as:

> *a construct used to describe policies and practices, especially with respect to school discipline, in the public schools and the juvenile justice system that decrease the probability of school success for children and youth, and increase the probability of negative life outcomes, particularly through involvement in the juvenile justice system.* (p. 546)

It's important to note that some scholars (e.g. Milner, Cunningham, Delale-O'Connor, & Gold Kestenberg, 2019) are now using the term Cradle-to-Prison Pipeline (CTPP) to describe the systemic oppression that many youths are facing both in and outside of schools. This term is important because it broadens the scope of the problem and points out the many systemic injustices that influence the lives of youth. Milner et al. (2019) define CTPP as:

> *A term that explicitly acknowledges that because of structural, systemic, institutional, and societal challenges and barriers that produce inequity, inequality, racism, and various other forms of discrimination, some students are pushed toward prison as soon as they are born.* (p. 33)

The CTPP disproportionately affects Black and Latinx youth from lower income families when compared with their upper class, white peers. As stated by Irizarry (2009):

*The increased hyper-vigilant surveillance of urban youth of color vividly demonstrated by the practice of placing police officers, security cameras, metal detectors and the like in schools, illustrates the mind-set and the role that schools play in contributing to and reifying the school-to-prison pipeline.* (p. 194)

Youth who experience increased involvement with law enforcement in schools are more likely to experience an increased involvement with law enforcement as adults. This phenomenon has been occurring in the United States' school system over the last few decades as a by-product of the "tough on crime" Reagan presidency (Alexander, 2010). The 1980s brought changes in policing across the country that, with it, brought changes in the schools. Ignited by the "war on drugs" and spurred through a media-induced fear of crime, upper class, white Americans were primed and ready for more stringent policing tactics—ones that predominantly affected the poor and people of color. Poor students and students of color were getting harsher punishments for the same crimes as those committed by their upper-class white peers (Milner et al., 2019). The discipline issues occurring within MLK seem to be a result of a larger national trend, considering that the school has one of the highest discipline rates in the school district (see Figure 1). The harsh discipline practices at MLK led the students to their first research topic, school discipline.

Figure 1: Discipline Data for 2016-2017

| **2016-2017 School Report Card Data** **153.5 discipline actions per 100 students** |
| --- |
| 417 occurrences of disobedient/disruptive behavior for ISS |
| 210 occurrences of fighting/violence for A2S/A2E |
| 13 occurrences of theft for A2S/A2E |
| 10 occurrences of use/possession of drugs for A2S/A2E |
| 57 occurrences of disobedient/disruptive behavior for A2S/A2E |
| 502 occurrences of disobedient/disruptive behavior for emergency removal |
| 10 occurrences of harassment/intimidation for emergency removal |
| 41 occurrences of fighting/violence for emergency removal |
| 47 occurrences of truancy for emergency removal |

Before delving into the research, the youth conducted on the discipline issues at their school, we should discuss the process we went through with the youth. YPAR is not a linear process. This kind of research is messy and takes time. Centering the knowledge and experience of youth requires some pre-work before delving into the research and action components. Building a sense of community and developing relationships among those contributing to the YPAR work is key to the success of the project (Mirra et al., 2016). When we come into communities looking to serve them, we are stepping into communities that are not our own, and it is our duty to gain the trust of the stakeholders of those communities and show that we value their stories and their culture. We sincerely hope our MLK High School mentors felt that we valued them as knowledgeable citizens.

Initial conversations were filled with silence and little participation from some of the youth mentors. Community building exercises included playing basketball, but that was not enough considering that most of our college mentee group was unathletic and did not enjoy any level of physical activity above the basic need to walk from the refrigerator to the sofa. During the beginning of this process we spent time engaging in general conversations just to get to know one another better. This included icebreaker activities and one-on-one conversations. To collect at least some information for future research, we decided to keep topics light and not delve into the deepest realms of social justice, because truthfully, our youth mentors did not trust us enough to let us know how they felt about their environment, specifically their high school, even though we were sure they were opinionated about how they were treated and how their school operated. It was not until our questions became personally introspective that our dialogue seemed to flow more, and we were able to find a topic that everyone wanted to work with. Instead of asking, "How are teachers at MLK," we switched the focus on the mentor and asked, "Why do you feel more connected to some teachers or classes versus others?" We also started to respond differently to them by asking them to delve deeper into an experience with a teacher, probing them with, "Why did you do or say that?" and continuing those kinds of conversations, instead of asking students about the school as a whole. We heard stories of teachers disrespecting students and students disrespecting teachers. The students told us about their experiences with in-school suspensions, out-of-school suspensions, and the almost constant threat of 3-day removal. Many of the students shared stories of how getting in trouble inside the school also involved trouble outside of school, peers getting into fights with each other, and police involvement. These testimonies correlated closely with the CTPP we were learning about in class and the grim realization that this was a reality for many of the students in the YPAR group. Given their personal experiences, the youth mentors decided to focus on the effectiveness of discipline policies at MLK for the YPAR project.

As the discussion process began, we dove into understanding the mentors' experience. Their teacher asked them to consider hard topics—like family violence and neighborhood safety—and formulate questions, ideas, and opinions. This was not difficult for the bright teenagers, many of whom had plenty of personal experience with the issues. Allowing the students to share their perspectives, unhinged and free flowing, gave us an opportunity to dissect the ways in which the students felt isolated in their own communities. The students shared stories of excessive punishment for minor incidents, racist teachers, and general disrespect in how they were treated in school. A reactionary response occurred as each student recounted the aggressive instances as daily interactions. We quickly realized that many teacher-student relationships were defined by hate and fear of the other. One of our students spoke about a time when a teacher reprimanded her for asking questions. The teacher accused her of talking back, which initiated a conflict, ending with the student feeling invalidated. This experience mirrors the discussion in the literature on the CTPP that points out that Black students are more likely to get in trouble for subjective behaviors than their white peers (Milner et al., 2019). Each interaction took something away from the students' confidence, leading them to disengage. This speaks to the cultural disconnect between many teachers and their students (Gay, 2014; Howard, 2006; Ladson-Billings 2000). We continued to engage in critical conversations with the youth during our school visits and our Saturday work sessions.

During activities in their classroom and group discussions on Saturday afternoons at the Peaslee Neighborhood Center, we could see the light switches going off in their heads during conversation and the passion brewing and growing inside them once they broke out of their shells. This came with time and often a change of approach. One thing we learned from this process is that *how* you ask people questions matters. They have the answers and solutions to problems, but you might have to change your perspective and frame your question differently in a way that makes better sense to them. Over the course of the semester—and even sometimes over the course of one afternoon visit—the quietest of the students would burst open with incredible insight and ideas for community solutions. Suddenly, their openness and bravery were glowing as an example to their peers that there was a lot more they could do in the classroom than sit there and try to look cool. Over the course of a few months, we spent time brainstorming ideas and collecting data about the discipline climate in the school. Coupled with increased conversation about the students' personal lives, by the end of the year, our MLK mentors became more comfortable working with us and sharing their ideas with us.

The actual YPAR project took a variety of twists and turns as we found that building relationships, working with other staff in the school building, and relying on teenagers to show up to meetings all presented unique challenges. We knew our group's work with the high school students from MLK would come with a set of challenges, but we were all taken aback when we realized just how *real* those challenges were going to be as we began collaborative classroom activities with them. As the high school students continued to discuss the discipline issues in their school, they began to think through how administration currently disciplines students and began brainstorming policy changes they would like to see implemented in their school. For example, if a student uses profanity towards a teacher, they are given a 3-day removal from school. The high school students and many of their peers feel as if this is an unjust punishment because it doesn't help the situation. There is no discussion of why the situation occurred, and there is no explicit reconciliation. In many cases, it just makes matters worse. Students are able to bring a parent or guardian to the school to have a conference with the assistant principal, and then they are allowed to come back before they have served their 3-day removal. However, not all parents or guardians are able to come to the school for a variety of reasons such as work, transportation, and child care needs. The high school students expressed how sending students out of school does not help the students or the school because most kids do not care about being suspended because they believe the school does not care. They explained how many kids who cuss out teachers, get into fights, skip class, gamble, etc., are the same kids always getting into trouble.

Conversations like these allowed our students to dream of new policies for the future to help keep students in school, which they believe will, ultimately, drastically lower discipline issues. They dreamt of ideas such as keeping kids in "school" but providing them alternative programming run by adults who deeply care for students. They expressed how many of their peers do not actually care for themselves and that they need to learn this sooner rather than later, or it will continue to lead to negative outcomes. In this particular dream for the future, students would still be provided an opportunity to complete their normal class work on top of an opportunity to better themselves in a building that is familiar to them with adults who are familiar to them. They also wanted student leaders to be a part of this program to help their peers. They said the students who did something that warranted being sent out of school would have to prove themselves in this program. They would have to show some type of personal growth or at least the willingness to want to do better. Then, if a student chose to continue to do wrong because they were not showing any signs of personal growth, they could be suspended from school. The YPAR students' thinking behind this notion was that people can only be helped so much. If someone does not want to help themselves when they have been provided the opportunity to help themselves, then that's their fault. They will have to deal with the negative consequences of their negative choices until they have their own personal wake-up call. They believe this program to be fair because it gives students the opportunity to transform themselves into more positive individuals, and if they choose to not take hold of that opportunity, even in the smallest way, then they deserve to try to work things out on their own with an actual suspension from school. In many ways, students were still struggling with the nuances between individual issues and large, structural problems that create systemic injustice. However, YPAR is a process and students are on different points of the path to becoming critically conscious.

Though the students had envisioned this dream, they immediately said it would never work because it would never happen. They knew the amount of planning, time, funding, and effort it would take to make a program such as this exist and be successful. It would take adults truly caring for students and the students would need to believe in themselves. This program would not be a quick "fix," in the same way that 3-day removals, suspensions, and expulsions are on paper. They had a negative attitude about something like this ever being implemented because they thought the administration would not be supportive.

This type of thinking led to them brainstorming what information they could provide to the administration to help demonstrate why a program like this was needed in the school. They decided to create a survey to give to their peers that asked questions about discipline policies and procedures. Then, they would show these results to the administration to make their case for policy changes. The creation of the survey was a lengthy process, and the implementation did not go as planned. There was not enough support from other teachers in the building to get the results the students wanted. The high school students had planned to survey most students in grades 7-12. They ended up receiving survey results from 148 students total from grades 7-12, which is a population of roughly 900 students. It is not a surprise that teachers did not support the project. When students seek to make change through YPAR "conflict can and often does emerge when educators seek to maintain the status quo while students begin to assert their voices to demand more from the institutions entrusted with their education" (Irizarry & Brown, 2014, p. 73). The survey results are included below and provide evidence of the discipline disparities at the school.

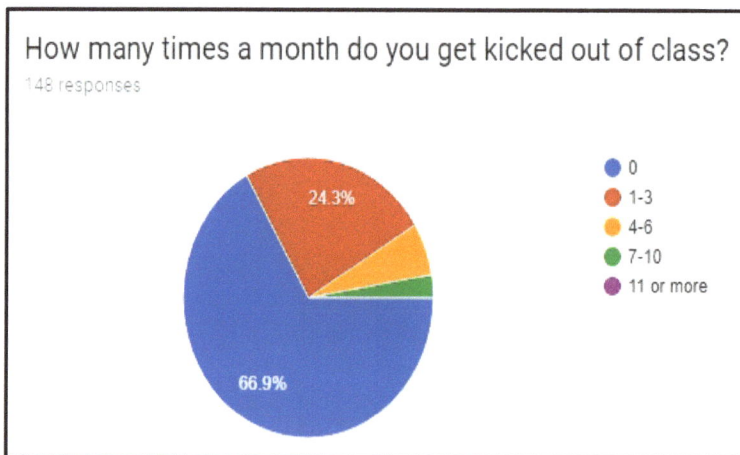

How many times a month do you get kicked out of class?
148 responses

- 0
- 1-3
- 4-6
- 7-10
- 11 or more

24.3%

66.9%

## How many of your current teachers do you think care about you?

148 responses

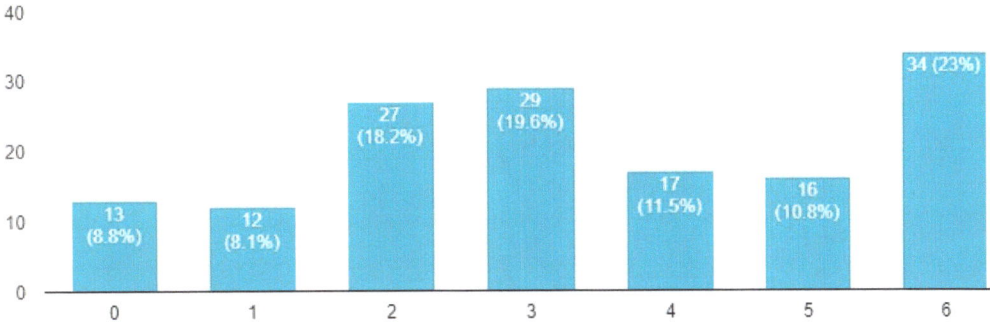

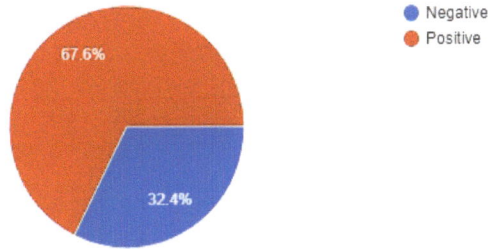

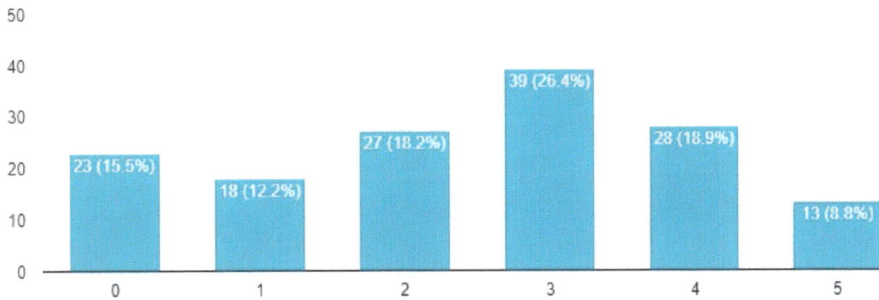

| Score | Count |
|-------|-------|
| 0 | 13 (8.8%) |
| 1 | 12 (8.1%) |
| 2 | 27 (18.2%) |
| 3 | 29 (19.6%) |
| 4 | 17 (11.5%) |
| 5 | 16 (10.8%) |
| 6 | 34 (23%) |

## In general, do you feel like your teachers' personalities affect you in a negative or positive way?

148 responses

- Negative — 32.4%
- Positive — 67.6%

## On a scale of 0 to 5 (0 being not effective at all and 5 being very effective), how effective/powerful are our various discipline policies?

148 responses

| Score | Count |
|-------|-------|
| 0 | 23 (15.5%) |
| 1 | 18 (12.2%) |
| 2 | 27 (18.2%) |
| 3 | 39 (26.4%) |
| 4 | 28 (18.9%) |
| 5 | 13 (8.8%) |

57

**Instead of receiving a 3 day removal for skipping class, do you think administration should ask why you aren't there first?**

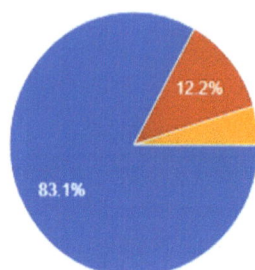

- Yes
- No
- It doesn't matter. Either way, I am still going to skip class whenever I want.

83.1%

12.2%

**Do you feel like you learn your lesson from getting suspended or put out of school or do you feel like you would learn you learn your lesson better from discussing the situation with a staff member?**

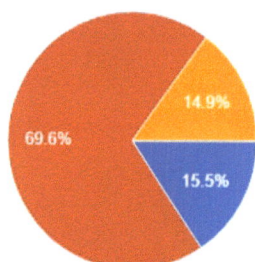

- I am more likely to learn my lesson by getting suspended/removal
- I am more likely to learn my lesson if I am required to discuss the situation with a staff member
- I never get suspended or put on removal.

69.6%

14.9%

15.5%

**How do you feel when you receive a 3 day removal?**

148 responses

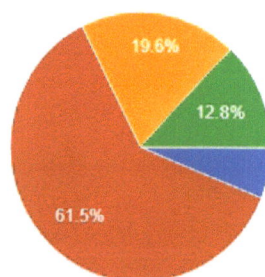

- I feel like I'm on a vacation. I look forward to it. It doesn't matter to me.
- It makes me angry because I'm going to miss out on my education.
- I don't care either way.
- I have never received a 3 day removal.

19.6%

12.8%

61.5%

If you're someone who consistently finds yourself in trouble, would it be helpful if you had one teacher who you could work with to help you stay out of trouble?

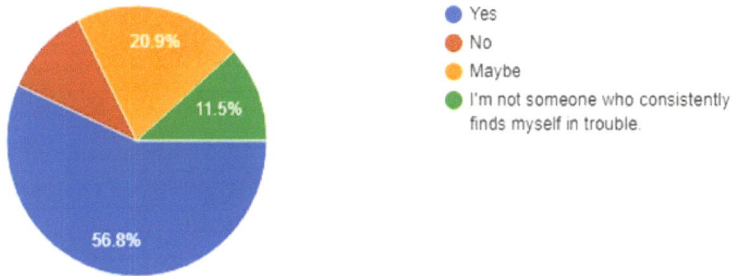

- Yes
- No
- Maybe
- I'm not someone who consistently finds myself in trouble.

20.9%
11.5%
56.8%

---

The consequences for fighting in your school are equal for all students.

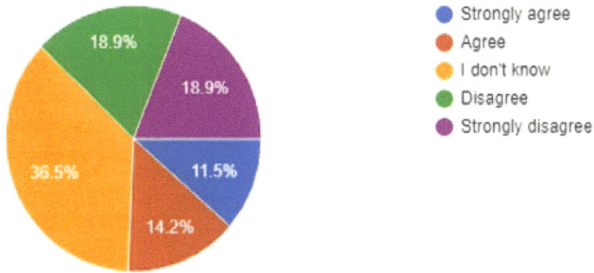

- Strongly agree
- Agree
- I don't know
- Disagree
- Strongly disagree

18.9%
18.9%
36.5%
11.5%
14.2%

---

How many people do you know who have gotten in a physical fight this school year over something that started on social media?

148 responses

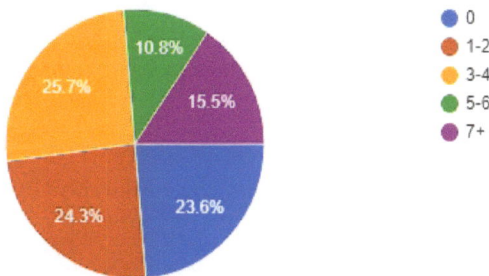

- 0
- 1-2
- 3-4
- 5-6
- 7+

10.8%
25.7%
15.5%
24.3%
23.6%

59

In addition to the quantitative survey data, students also collected qualitative data by having participants respond to the following prompt:

> *Please provide any feedback about the discipline policies here at MLK. For example, what is your opinion of them? Do they work? What would you like to see changed? What could we as students do to also help make our school even better?*

Students who responded to the qualitative portion of the survey fell into a few different categories. Some of the students pointed out that there needed to be some kind of discussion with students who were breaking the rules:

| | |
|---|---|
| *I don't think suspensions are working, most students look at it as time off of school. They should just have a conversation with the student about what happened.* | *I think that the discipline policies are not fair in some cases and they do not work because there are still people that argue even when the conflict is over. I would like to see them talk the problem out instead of just kicking them out of school. I don't think the students can help that much with the problem, but the students can be more considerate about the fight or argument and not get loud and crazy.* |
| *I don't think they would change it but I think instead of telling the students can't come back they should talk with the students and parents of why they behave this way and how they can change for the better.* | |

Other students expressed clear frustration with the teachers and their seeming lack of care for students:

| | |
|---|---|
| *All this shit stupid and it don't matter because y'all don't really care about us anyways* | *I think timeout is stupid because it doesn't do anything but piss us off.* |
| *Sometimes they work. I would like to see change in the way teachers talk to the students.* | *For this generation or era of students, I think the staff, teachers* |

| | |
|---|---|
| I think they should find out what teachers really want to teach because some of them do not care about the students. | should connect & build with the students more on a personal and academic level to understand and help with students behavior and also probably academically. |
| The staff need to change. | They don't work and y'all show favoritism towards athletes. |

On the other hand, some students blamed the attitudes and behaviors of their peers and suggested their peers needed to do the work:

| | |
|---|---|
| I feel that some of the discipline policies are reasonable and I feel some policies are not. Some discipline policies are effective and some are not because some students don't care and continue to do the same bad habits. | |
| They are okay, they don't always work and we can do our work and stop getting in trouble. | I feel it's stupid like the kids don't care about their future anyway so even if it does change they won't. |
| I would like to change my peers. They are very disrespectful to the people that are trying to help us the most other than our parents. | I don't think they work because when we get suspended we just come back with the same attitude. |

A few of the students pointed out the absurdity of students being sent away from school and learning opportunities. They suggested that students get some kind of in school punishment instead of being suspended:

| | |
|---|---|
| They always cry to our parents about how we never in class, never at school, they want us to be in class each and everyday, etc. But as soon as something happen they automatically gives us days instead of suspending us, there is in school suspension for a reason. Our school don't use that room for nothing...start putting us in I.S.S. that way we're still in school and able to work. | I feel instead of kicking students out of class and suspending student give them more time in school like Saturday school and detentions to keep them in school not out. |
| | I hate that we get three days for skipping that's stupid because that's taking the student away from even more learning. |

This student discussed the harm of the policies and the real lack of concern for the problems students are facing, both from staff and peers. It is clear this student wants to see change and knows some of their peers are hurting:

> *The policies are kind of dumb sometimes such as automatic 3 days if your skipping class. What if something happened what if the person had a massive problem or trying to avoid someone for a hour. We could make teachers actually help us and listen to us. But nooo they want to always kick us out of class when something is bothering us bad. And it's a shame. We as students can help each other out come together and stop laughing at other students when they come to class crying because something bad happened at home and they can't hold back the tears. We can also try to stop being so mean. Students are always mean for no reason and it's sad.*

After the completion of the survey, winter break was upon us, then standardized testing season, and the beginning of the end of the school year hit us. Unfortunately, acting on the results of the survey as the students originally planned did not happen due to a variety of factors. We learned that more time and authentic participation is needed to carry out such a project to achieve the desired results. It is our hope that, in the future, the survey results will help turn our dream of the program described above into an actual program in the school.

Over time, the focus of our groups' work changed from research and immediate change to activism and creating a peer support system, with some students drifting in and out of the group. These inconsistencies were frustrating, making it seem like we were making little progress in our YPAR work. However, these challenges strengthened our group in terms of patience and flexibility in the face of adversity—skills that will benefit each of us as individuals for the rest of our lives, too. At the end of the semester, a video was created to share at our final retreat. The youth in the YPAR group were asked to respond to the following prompt:

> *What would you like to say to someone or some system that is attempting to oppress you?/What would you want to say to your oppressor?*

The two images below are examples of images used in the video.

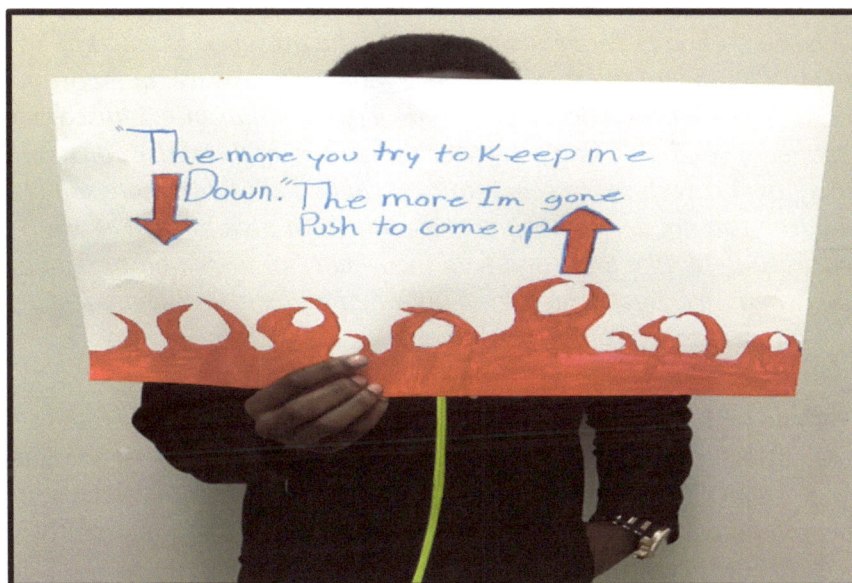

## Reflections from the Mentees

The college student mentees were impacted by their work with the youth mentors. Here are a few of examples provided by three of the college student mentees. The first example highlights how the school-to-prison pipeline is a phenomenon that this student experienced first-hand but was unaware of at the time. The YPAR work has also prompted this student to figure out ways to incorporate YPAR projects into his future career.

> *The YPAR work has opened my eyes to how much of the discipline that many of my peers went through wasn't fair and pushed them out of success when they were smart, competent students. It was shocking to me because I was unaware of the problems even though they were taking place in my K-12 schools. Secondly, it made me want to explore how YPAR can be regularly used in high schools through extra-curricular clubs. This is something I plan to do in my future work.*

The second example provides evidence of the way this college student's perception of youth changed over the course of this project. This honest reflection is a powerful testament to the importance of projects that promote relationships and community building amongst people who might not otherwise collaborate.

> *The YPAR work really impacted my view of the importance of youth. To be honest, I had never really considered the presence of youth to be an asset to a community. It wasn't that I thought kids were unimportant— most of the work I do is centered around children!—I just hadn't thought of youth as being framed in the context of the entire community. This flaw in my thinking seems to be a reflection of the whole society— children are not seen as important enough to give back. The truth is, when we think like that (and feed them that lie), they don't give back. But, when we expect them to step up, when we instill value in them, they give more than we could ever imagine!*

The third example highlights the issue the youth were working to address in their school and how this particular white college student had a different experience in school. Her words point to the power of YPAR to change the perspectives of college students and to challenge them to take a closer look at their privilege. But most importantly you feel her empathy for the students in this statement.

*Working with the high schoolers through YPAR was a much more emotional experience than I had expected it to be. Seeing the extremely high levels of security and the lack of trust the faculty and staff had in the students was disheartening and opened my eyes to how the freedom my teachers gave me in high school shaped me as a young adult and prepared me for the next chapters of my life. These intelligent, growing individuals are deprived of responsibility and independence because it is assumed that they will wrongly take advantage of it. Teachers expect they will squander opportunities rather than rightly take advantage of them. When they do make mistakes, they are often punished without anyone asking after their mental health, what's happening at home, or what drove them to act the way they did. How will their minds and spirits grow if they are never allowed trust? How will they believe in themselves if their teachers and role models do not believe in them? This is an element of education I had never considered before being involved in YPAR but that I now see is critical to student success. These teenagers taught me more than I ever imagined and brought both my privilege and the dire need for change in urban schools to light.*

The YPAR work also had an impact on the youth mentors. Their teacher conveyed what the YPAR work meant to her students.

*YPAR was an incredible experience for my students. Each student grew academically as well as personally. Students learned how to better use their voices and their minds to interact with the world around them with the purpose of enacting positive change. Mentoring college students empowered my high school students because they were viewed as the experts. They felt valued in knowing they have knowledge and experiences that were able to help and guide others. Though the work of creating a more student-centered and student-focused school environment is ongoing, this project propelled new ways of thinking and acting throughout our school. Students were able to provide their input and know their voices were being valued.*

This chapter is a testament to the value of using YPAR with youth so that they realize the power they have to push for change in their communities and schools. Although we did not get to implement the new discipline approach the students came up with, the work was still powerful and meaningful to both the youth mentors and the college student mentees. This experience will shape and inform the practices of the college students as they step into their careers as teachers, public health practitioners, and psychologists. This work also helped the high school youth tap into their own power and will hopefully continue to inform their education and personal experiences. The current, zero-tolerance approach to discipline used in many urban schools today must be disrupted if we hope to put a stop to the CTPP. YPAR is an approach to curriculum and research that provides youth the opportunity to push for this change alongside their teachers and other critically conscious comrades who are committed to schools that are more just and equitable.

# References

Alexander, M. (2016). *The new Jim Crow: Mass incarceration in the age of colorblindness.* New York, NY: New Press.

Burke, K. J., Greene, S., & McKenna, M. K. (2017). Youth voice, civic engagement and failure in participatory action research. *Urban Review, 49,* 585-601.

Cammarota, J., & Fine, M. (2008). *Revolutionizing education: Youth participatory action research in motion.* New York, NY: Routledge.

Fine, M., Tuck, E., & Young, K. W. (2014). An intimate memoir of resistance theory. In E. Tuck & K. W. Yang (Eds.), *Youth resistance research and theories of change* (pp. 46-58). New York, NY: Routledge.

Freire, P. (1970). *Pedagogy of the oppressed.* New York, NY: Continuum.

Freire, P., & Macedo, D. (1987). *Literacy: Reading the word and the world.* South Hadley, MA: Bergin & Garvey.

Gay, G. (2014). Culturally responsive teaching principles, practices, and effects. In H. R. Milner, IV, and K. Lomotey (Eds.), *The handbook of urban education* (pp. 353-372). London, UK: Routledge.

Grace, S., & Langhout, R. D. (2014). Questioning our questions: Assessing question asking practices to evaluate a YPAR program. *The Urban Review, 46,* 703-724.

Howard, G. R. (2006). We can't teach what we don't know: White teachers, multiracial schools. New York, NY: Teachers College, Columbia University.

Irizarry, J. G. (2009). Reinvigorating multicultural education through youth participatory action research. *Multicultural Perspectives, 11*(4), 194-199.

Irizarry, J. G., & Brown, T. M. (2014). Humanizing research in dehumanizing spaces: The challenges and opportunities of conducting participatory action research with youth in schools. In D. Paris & M. T. Winn (Eds.), *Humanizing research: Decolonizing qualitative inquiry with youth and communities* (pp. 63-80). Thousand Oaks, CA: Sage.

Kohfeldt, D., Bowen, A. R., & Langhout, R. D. (2016). "The think kids are stupid": YPAR and confrontations with institutionalized power as contexts for children's identity work. *Puerto Rican Journal of Psychology/Revista Puertorriqueña De Psicología, 27*(2), 276-291.

Ladson-Billings, G. (2000). Fighting for our lives: Preparing teachers to teach African American students. *Journal of Teacher Education, 51*(3), 206-214.

Milner, R. H., Cunningham, H. B., Delale-O'Connor, & L., Gold Kestenberg, E. (2019). *"These kids are out of control": Why we must reimagine "classroom management" for equity.* Thousand Oaks, CA: Corwin.

Mirra, N., Garcia A., and Morrell, E. (2016). *Doing youth participatory action research: Transforming inquiry with researchers, educators, and students.* New York, NY: Routledge.

Nocella, A. J., Parmar, P., & Stovall, D. (2014). *From education to incarceration: Dismantling the school-to-prison pipeline.* New York, NY: Peter Lang.

Scott, M. A., Pyne, K. B., & Means, D. R. (2015). Approaching praxis: yPAR as critical pedagogical process in a college access program. *The High School Journal, 98,* 138-157.

Skiba, R. J., Arredondo, M. I., & Williams, N. T. (2014). More than a metaphor: The contribution of exclusionary discipline to a school-to-prison pipeline. *Equity & Excellence in Education, 47,* 546-564.

# Interlude

## YPAR Project Introduction: Lilyfield

By Heather Allentuck Davis, teacher

*Here's a bit of love*
*Here's a little trust*
*Here's some love*
*Lotta love right now*
-Truce- Nathan Nzanga

The song "Truce" by Nathan Nzanga became one of the theme songs for our Youth Participatory Action Research (YPAR) work. We listened to it when we needed inspiration, when we were starting our day, and then ended up using it as the background for our final collaborative action. We all need a little love. YPAR is all about love.

I am a graduate of Miami University and was also a part of the Urban Cohort (UC). When I first joined the UC as a student at Miami, we started the year with an introductory retreat. Ms. Dorothy, one of the UC matriarchs, was asked to give us some advice to help start us on our journey to becoming community teachers. Her reply was that sometimes you just need to "go wash your face." It took a little while to figure out exactly what she meant, but since then, those words have stuck with me. When you wake up in the morning, you wash your face to help you start your day well. When you are having a bad moment, wash your face and then keep going. Even when we've made a mess, we can wash our faces and keep going, keep struggling for change alongside our students. The work of the Urban Cohort goes beyond just curriculum. When we met, we always sat in a circle. As Dr. Tammy explained to the group the very first time we met, we sit in a circle because it makes us all equal. No one is in front or behind; everyone's an expert on something; everyone has something valuable to share. Because of my experiences with YPAR and the Urban Cohort, this principle also makes its way into my teaching.

I am now a middle school math teacher at Lilyfield School. The school of Lilyfield itself is growing. Three years ago, we had about 350 students, we are now pushing 500. Lilyfield is a prek-8 school. The school has neighborhood students, a large portion of the district's students with multiple disabilities, as well as a growing refugee program. Our student demographics make Lilyfield a unique school with many strengths and also many challenges. I decided to partner with Miami University because of my own ties to the Urban Cohort Program and the transformative potential of YPAR work.

In the era of test-focused teaching and high stakes accountability, sometimes it is hard to teach in context. As a math teacher, I feel pressured to make sure students know the content, and it is difficult to think about the real-world application of math concepts when there is so much emphasis placed on testing. The Urban Cohort challenges me to be a community teacher and to make connections between my curriculum and the lived experiences of my students.

Peter Murrell (2001) defines a community teacher as "an accomplished practitioner who is culturally connected with students, families and communities in ways that have yet to be articulated by any of the plethora of professional teaching standards" (p. 2). In addition, a community teacher "possesses and works to build on his/her contextualized knowledge of culture, community and the identity of children and families as the core of his/her teaching practice" (Murrell, 2001, p. 2). The context of the community needs to be integrated into the curriculum. YPAR provides an opportunity to make these meaningful curricular and community connections. YPAR is not just something I do with students after school hours, but the way I embody teaching. For example, when I teach the area of shapes in 6th grade, instead of just learning the area formulas, doing some practice, taking a quiz and then moving on, we participate in a community project. Students were complaining about how there was not a lot of space to play in the neighborhood and how there was a lot of empty space behind the school where there used to be a swimming pool. Students used Google Maps to measure the area behind the park, brainstormed and interviewed others about what they would like to see in the park, and then designed it. Finally, students found the area of everything they created in their park and created a budget.

While students were engaged in the project, I questioned if students thought the project was important. How could I have actually had them present their ideas to community council? Could they have actually built their parks? Would administrators understand why doing projects like this is important and not see it as time wasted that could be spent on test prep? Thinking of curriculum as community-based is challenging. It requires thinking beyond the pacing guide and textbook. It requires listening, thinking critically, and asking questions. There are not a ton of resources available for ideas or lesson plans. However, I do not think there should be ready made curriculum for this type of pedagogy. Every community is different, every context is different, and therefore, place-based curriculum should not be cookie-cuttered into schools. It requires you to fight—fight for what is best for STUDENTS, which often requires challenging the status quo. Community teaching requires love, love for the students, love for community, and love for teaching. Our YPAR project is grounded in love.

For our project, we chose violence as our focus. When we sat down to make the decision about what we were going to study, we had just experienced several lockdowns because of the violence occurring close to the school. While discussing why students wanted to pick this topic, they told stories about how they could not sleep certain nights because of the violence they heard outside on the street. Some of the students shared stories about witnessing or hearing about someone they know getting injured or killed. Violence was very present in their lives and weighed heavy on their hearts and minds. The YPAR project provided a space for students to begin to process the pain of these experiences and to work towards action to change these conditions.

This year was my first year leading a YPAR group. When I was a student in the Urban Cohort, we worked with a group of students at Urban Elementary (one of the schools featured in this book) and discussed social justice issues, but we did not follow the YPAR structure. Most of the YPAR work this past year felt messy. But, I think YPAR is meant to be messy. What we were researching was not black and white, but rather many shades of grey. There is no one answer to why violence exists, nor is there only one solution. Throughout the year, we read articles, watched videos, had discussions, and wrote about the issue. One of the struggles the students had was that they did not feel like they could eradicate violence. I saw them gain more confidence in themselves, their voices. They shared their opinions more not only during YPAR but at school. When the students saw an injustice at school, the YPAR students rallied some of the other middle school students to fight what they believed was wrong. They even convinced their ELA teacher to let them discuss their opinions on issues that concerned them in their argumentative essays. Prior to the YPAR work, I rarely saw students use their voices in this manner.

Our YPAR cycle is one school year. We met twice a month on Saturdays for four hours each time. One of our biggest frustrations was that we felt like we did not have enough time to do everything we wanted to do. The more the students studied violence, the more they realized how complicated their topic really was. They quickly realized that the solution to violence would have to be multi-faceted. Some students focused on violence that is due to drugs. They brainstormed that students need a different type of drug education. Other students focused on violence due to poverty. They discovered that there are barriers to people being able to get jobs and wanted to create more job programs like Venice of Vine (see chapter for more details). They struggled with figuring out how to create a product for the final UC retreat that happens at the end of each year to show their findings, but also a product that would help cause real change. In the end, they created a Public Service Announcement with the message that there is violence, that it affects youth, and that the violence is not acceptable. We showed the video at the Urban Cohort final retreat and to the entire middle school at Lilyfield. Students wanted to show it to the community council, but we could not get on the board minutes, I think if we had more time, through either more meetings, or working together for more than a year, students would have taken the project further and would have been able to implement some of their other ideas. For future projects, I hope that we can extend this work and make it more long-term.

71

All pre-service teachers should participate in YPAR with students before having their own classrooms. To do YPAR successfully, you need to learn to build positive relationships with the youth. Building strong and positive relationships with students is a key factor to having a safe and productive classroom. YPAR also encourages viewing communities from an asset perspective and helps to disrupt deficit narratives about urban schools, communities, and students. Even if preservice teachers do not teach in the same community in which they do YPAR, the belief of community as an asset can carry them far in the communities where they live and work in the future. This approach to curriculum and pedagogy gives teachers the tools to challenge the status quo and to do so alongside their students.

*Give a bit of love*
*Give a little love*
*Give some love*
*Gotta love right now*
*No more pain in my heart*
*We're the same in my heart*
*Start the chain of the change right now*
-Truce- Nathan Nzanga

# References

Murrell, P. C., Jr. (2001). *Community teacher: A new framework for effective urban teaching.* New York, NY: Teachers College Press.

Nzanga, N. (2016). Truce (mp3 recording). Seattle, WA: JIMZ Entertainment. Retrieved from https://soundcloud.com/nathannzanga/truce

# Chapter 4:
## The Kings and Queens of Lilyfield School: The Power of Coming to Voice

By  Maria Kahn, Monica Parsley, Taylor Hayes, Samantha Crozier

When we first met our youth mentors on that warm September day, we knew this was going to be a great experience. Looking back at that day, and everything else in between, we have seen the growth that each one of our mentors has undergone. They are more comfortable speaking up in our group, smile bigger, laugh louder, and are eager to chase their dreams. To those who say that the youth aren't powerful, we dare them to meet the kings and queens of Lilyfield School.

One of the strengths of Youth Participatory Action Research (YPAR) is that it helps youth understand the power and strength of their voices (Morrell, 2006; Strobel, Osberg, & McLaughlin, 2006). Their voices have the potential and power to reach and mobilize people of all ages, genders, religions, and races. Youth engaged in this work "build on powerful, organic histories of resistance and cultural wealth" (Mirra, Garcia, & Morrell, 2016, p. 63). The youth are the future, and how they engage in the struggle for justice matters. As "scholars-in-process," they can change lives and flip the status quo; we just have to listen with open hearts and minds (Nieto, 2018, p. xvi). Prior to our first meeting Ms. Heather Allentuck Davis, our collaborating teacher, gave us a list of information that our mentors wanted us to know about themselves and their school. One of the most important items on that list was the school mascot and motto—the lion and the "Lion's Roar." Similar to their school motto and mascot, the students have powerful voices. This served as a powerful metaphor throughout our time working with the youth.

When we first began meeting, the Lilyfield students were pretty quiet, but that did not mean that they didn't have anything to say. They needed to be asked, and they needed to feel safe to enter the room and to share their ideas. Once they realized that we were there to listen and that we were actually going to hear them, they never stopped talking. They just needed to be reassured that, "We hear you, we are with you, and we want to learn from you." This required developing meaningful relationships with the youth in order to build trust and create a space for dialogue. One of our favorite memories in creating these relationships was a morning of basketball at the community courts across from Urban Elementary. Despite our lack of coordination, we played with smiles on our faces and tears from laughter in our eyes until it was time to head back to Peaslee, the local community center where we met one Saturday a month, for an afternoon of critical thought. Sometimes building community means being playful and finding joy in our everyday experiences. There is joy, hope, and love in each one of us and in our relationships with one another. As stated by hooks, "Given the interdependent nature of our lives, of life on the planet, to share in communal encounter is vital for our survival. But the joy we share must come from within, must be rooted in our own soulfulness " (p. 229). Before moving on to discuss the details of our YPAR project, it's important to position ourselves within this work.

## The Mentors
## (mentors names have been replaced with pseudonyms)

❖ Jamal is a small, quiet sixth grader with the mind of someone much older than himself. When given the space to think and the attention and patience from others, he speaks words that will shake you.

❖ Lamar speaks quickly and dreams big. His ideas are vast and never-ending, and you find yourself thinking about the successful future that this young man will have as he grows up, hoping that he never loses his imagination.

❖ David is daring and brave. He has a big heart and a bright mind and wants to do big things. He sees truth, even when it's a bit dark. I wouldn't be surprised to see him running for president one day.

❖ Kayla is extremely smart but struggles with self-confidence in school. She wants to do well, and when pushed, she exceeds her own expectations. Over the course of this year, she has not only started to find her voice, but has realized the power of her voice.

❖ Arianna may be small, but she is oh so mighty. She is one of the most energetic of the group and always has something to say. She feels deeply and runs wild. I hope she holds onto that fearless stride.

❖ Kayonna is reserved and mature. She is very self-aware and a dedicated student full of warmth and love. She is especially kind and has a heart of gold.

❖ Deandra has a deep sense of reality. She sees the world for what it is and doesn't sugar coat anything. She is quiet, but when she has something to say, everyone better listen up. She is 13 going on 30 and ready to shout the truth.

## Mentees

❖ My name is Maria, and I am one of the Urban Cohort mentees who had the wonderful opportunity to work alongside these incredible youth. I come from an upper middle-class family from a suburb of Chicago. I identify as an interfaith, Mexican American woman. And although I was born in the United States, my mother is Mexican, and my father is white.

❖ My name is Taylor, and I am one of the mentees who had the honor to work with the students of Lilyfield School. Building relationships with my mentors was one of my most cherished experiences to date, and I am grateful to them for allowing me to see a piece of their world. I come from an upper middle-class family from a suburb of Columbus, Ohio, and identify as a white and Christian woman.

❖ My name is Sam, and I am one of the mentees who had the opportunity to work with youth from Lilyfield through YPAR work. I am from an upper-middle class family in Columbus, and the time I spent with the Urban Cohort opened my eyes to the world of privilege and oppression.

❖ My name is Monica, and I am an Urban Cohort mentee who worked with the students from Lilyfield School. Doing YPAR with these students was an amazing experience that I, as a future teacher, learned so much from. I come from an upper middle-class family from the town of Loveland, Ohio. I am a white woman who first came to college knowing very little about social justice and YPAR work. While there is still much for me to learn, I feel that this YPAR experience has influenced my knowledge of issues of power, privilege, and oppression.

## Our YPAR Project: Community Violence and Safety in Lilyfield School

We began our YPAR work by brainstorming with our youth mentors about what they see and hear in their school, homes, and community. We placed chart paper around the room labeled school, home, and community. The students wrote down words, phrases, and activities they see and/or hear in each context. As the students began to identify different issues from their brainstorming, drugs and violence were recurring themes that came up in our conversations, so we decided to focus our project on those issues. During each Saturday session at Peaslee, we discussed crime rates, drug use, mass incarceration, and the war on drugs. Throughout the semester, we continued to have conversations about what we might do to address the violence and drug use in their community, but once the second semester started, there was a shift in the conversation. As the year progressed and we moved forward, we noticed that we were stuck. The mentors seemed to be losing heart, and as a result, we were losing heart too. We decided to pause and think about what was going on. We came to the conclusion that, because we were focusing so much on community deficits, we were ignoring the rich community assets within the neighborhood and city at large. During the last couple of months of our YPAR work, we decided to spend more time focusing on the strengths, assets, and the beautiful potential of this transformative work. We specifically wanted to seek out the "community cultural wealth" that communities of color tap into in order to thrive and survive in spaces that were not created with their needs in mind (Yosso, 2005). One way we did this was by interviewing a local business in Over-the-Rhine. Our trip to Venice on Vine, a local pizza place and caterer, exemplified the hard work that individuals are putting into the communities they care about in order to combat larger systemic issues.

In preparation for this visit, we took care of the logistical end of things, while the youth mentors did the bulk of the work by creating interview questions and facilitating the interviews that took place at Venice of Vine (See Figure 1). As stated on their website:

> *Venice on Vine is a pre-employment training and job placement program, for individuals with barriers to employment, that utilizes both a traditional pizzeria and a commercial catering kitchen as unique classrooms. The organization has functioned for more than 30 years within Cincinnati's urban core, the historic Over-the-Rhine district, under the umbrella of the non-profit Power Inspires Progress.* (PIP, 2018)

The youth mentors had a chance to interview the founders of Venice on Vine and to ask questions about their approach to helping people get back on their feet. In addition, they were able to interview an employee who was currently taking part in the training program offered at Venice on Vine.

Figure 1: Interview Questions

| **Questions for the founders** |
| --- |
| 1. How did your program start? |
| 2. What is your program about, and what do you do? |
| 3. Have you shared your program with other groups? |
| 4. Have there ever been problems with some of the people you have hired, because they have just come from jail? |
| |
| **Questions for one of the employees** |
| 5. How long have you been trying to get a job? |
| 6. Do you think that Venice On Vine is a good idea? |
| 7. Was your crime a big deal?---↓↓↓(then ask this) <br> From your crime, do you think that it will be harder to get a job? |
| 8. What is your dream job?---↓↓↓(then ask this) <br> Do you think what you did in the past prevented you from having your dream job? |
| 9. What do you think you can do to be able to get higher level skills? |

Leaving the pizza place, we felt a sense of hope, and I could see it in the eyes of the youth mentors as well. Their eyes were huge with interest—as if they were having a little epiphany moment. This led to our YPAR topic converting from violence and drugs to "building a better community." Moving forward, our conversations ended on a positive, motivating note. We thought about ways we could inform the people around us that there is joy and there is hope—we just have to keep our eyes and our hearts open to it.

Through this work, we realized an important truth—YPAR is messy. There is no rule book. There is no guide or easy, ready-made recipe for this work. You just have to jump into the water, feet first, and trust that the rest will follow. That is exactly what happened with the mighty youth of Lilyfield, and we will forever deeply value the time we had with them. We learned so much from our youth mentors over the course of the year we spent together. As stated by Freire (1998):

> *There is no valid teaching from which there does not emerge something learned and through which the learner does not become capable of recreating and remaking what has been thought. In essence, teaching that does not emerge from the experience of learning cannot be learned by anyone.* (p. 31)

These next sections discuss some of what we learned through this transformative and collaborative journey.

**Sticks and Stones May Break My Bones…but Names Will Damage My Self-Worth**

Part of the reason why youth do not understand the power of their voices is because of the systemic, often unexamined, oppression they face in their daily lives. YPAR provides a space for youth to understand the power of their voices and to interrogate the systemic oppression that has stifled their ability to push back against the status quo (Cammarota & Fine, 2008). In addition, "YPAR teaches young people that conditions of injustice are produced, not natural; are designed to privilege and oppress; but are ultimately challengeable and thus changeable" (Cammarota & Fine, 2008, p. 2). Most people have heard the iconic saying, "Sticks and stones may break my bones, but names will never hurt me." This little rhyme is typically used as a way to reassure the victims of name-calling that insults will never cause any physical pain. While it is true that negative words cannot physically harm someone, they can do long-term harm to self-efficacy and self-esteem. This can have a lasting impact on academic and life successes. It's common to think that name-calling gets left behind in the chaotic, hormone-filled world of grade school, but that is not the case. The destructive power of words persists in the adult world where it transforms into stereotyping, something that is used widely by adults and media outlets everywhere. As pointed out by Solorzano and Yosso (2001), teachers and teacher educators often use code words to perpetuate deficit laden stereotypes about students from lower socio-economic status backgrounds and students of color. Terms such as "uneducable" may be used in replacement of words such as "dumb, dirty or lazy" (p. 5). These seemingly juvenile habits of name calling are part of larger systems of oppression such as racism, classism, ableism, and heterosexism. These intertwined systems of oppression have a direct impact on the lives of young people and persist into adulthood, limiting access to resources, often leading people to believe the stereotypes that have been socially constructed to other and marginalize.

*The New Jim Crow* by Michelle Alexander (2010) captures the harm and lasting damage that racism and other forms of oppression can inflict:

> *All your life you been taught that you're not a worthy person, or something is wrong with you. So you don't have no respect for yourself. See, people of color have—not all of them, but a lot of them—have poor self-esteem, because we've been branded. We hate ourselves, you know. We have been programmed that it's something wrong with us. We hate ourselves.* (p. 168)

The systemic racism embedded in all of our institutions creates conditions in which many people blame themselves for the impact the system has on their lives. Systemic racism is further reinforced through racist depictions of the inner city in pop culture and media representations. Think of every inner city set (coded as ghetto) movie, every crime report on the news station, every episode of *The Wire*. What do these things have in common? What group of people are most often portrayed as the "bad" guys, the criminals, the addicts, the uneducated, and those deemed unworthy? People of color are portrayed in ways that reinforce a single, racist narrative that gets applied to all people within that racial group. These narratives reinforce the racist beliefs that have been perpetuated and reinforced by a society that is governed by white supremacy. We define white supremacy as "a sociopolitical economic system of domination based on racial categories that benefits those defined and perceived as white" (DiAngelo, 2018, p. 30), which creates conditions for the "pervasive and persistent reproduction of white people's values and attitudes in social norms and practices" (Florence, 1998, p. 13).

Urban, majority African American communities are often portrayed in the news or media as run down, dilapidated, and in need of fixing. There is a narrative that crime runs rampant on the streets, and the only ones who inhabit the area are drug addicts and "welfare queens." The various forms of institutional violence the Black community has faced since the inception of our country are not brought to bear on these deficit laden conversations (Dutton, 2001). Not once is the vibrant culture, sense of community, or rich and complex history mentioned, and very rarely are actual residents interviewed for their input on why they like living in their community. What kind of impact might these stereotypes and deficit narratives have on urban communities and the people who live in these communities? How would this affect the development of a young person living in a community that was considered to be the bad part of town or the wrong side of the tracks? Is it possible for youth to grow up to have respect for themselves and their community if they constantly receive the message that they're no good and where they live is a bad place? These questions are pertinent to our work with the youth mentors.

We've seen the effects of the deficit-laden stereotypes in the very students with whom we've worked through the YPAR process at Lilyfield School. As a part of the Urban Cohort Program at Miami University, we learn about and then try to educate people/students about urban communities and dispel the stereotypes of urban neighborhoods being crime ridden, run-down, and full of criminals. At first, the students wanted to make a PSA focusing on the violence and lack of safety that they believed existed in their community. Together, the youth mentors and the four college student mentees spent time doing extensive research on drug related issues that were prevalent in the community and how violence affects families. Through this process, we found various statistics on drug use, violence, and crime rates in the community surrounding the school. While researching these statistics, the students did not seem shocked by or interested in the information they were finding. At first, we assumed that it was solely because the work was monotonous, and the students were bored. However, after asking the students what they thought about the work they were doing and why they chose it, we all realized the monotony of the work wasn't the only factor. When asked why the students chose to title their project "Violence and Safety in the Community," their responses seemed to echo almost the exact words of what uninformed media and news outlets would project on tv screens across Cincinnati. The overall consensus of the students' perceptions of their community could be summed up as, "It's a bad place with bad people." It made us sad and angry when we began to understand that the middle school students believed that their neighborhoods were bad places.

After researching the effects of white supremacy and oppression in Empower I and II, the first-year seminars we take in the Urban Cohort, we learned that what was occurring within our students was internalized oppression. Internalized oppression is "internalizing and acting out (often unintentionally) the constant messages that you and your group are inferior to the dominant group and thus deserving of your lower position" (Sensoy & DiAngelo, 2012, p. 72). One of the Miami students in our group wondered how the deficit narratives that our students had bought into about their community impacted how they think about themselves. Do they believe that, because someone on tv says they live in a bad neighborhood, that they, by default, are bad as well?

It is tempting for one to think, "This is ridiculous; how can something a few news outlets or MTV 'reality' TV shows portray have an impact on ALL students? That's just not realistic. I mean I watched those things, and I'm not racist/I don't think I'm a bad person." Unfortunately, the effect of negative stereotypes on self-efficacy are not always obvious. According to Olson and Appunn (2017), self-efficacy "addresses how individuals perceive and interpret external sources related to self-understanding" (p. 59). One of our group members, Monica, recounted her experience seeing the effects of this negative stereotype on a 7th grade student at Lilyfield School.

This particular student was notorious in the school for not doing his work or paying attention during class. He was a known as a troublemaker to many of the teachers. One day during English class, Monica recalls going over to the student and asking why he wasn't working on his essay. Before the student had a chance to respond, his nearest classmate spoke up saying that the student never did any work and was just lazy. The student didn't answer for himself. He just sat there quietly as his peer continued talking. Monica prompted the student to go get a computer and start working on his essay. He was reluctant to work, complaining about how he hadn't done any work and how there was no way he would finish his essay by the end of the bell. Monica ignored his complaints and instead encouraged and prompted him to work on his essay.

Monica noted that, at first, the student was overwhelmed with all the work there was to complete, but with every sentence he wrote, and every paragraph completed, he became less overwhelmed and prouder of what he had accomplished. Monica helped him brainstorm key points in the essay and encouraged him to do the work. Everything else he was able to do on his own, and by the end of the class period, he had completed the essay. When he was finished, he kept saying he would have never been able to complete his essay if Monica hadn't been there. Monica admitted that she had played a minimal role in helping the student. The main struggle the student had with writing was grammar, which was an easy fix. When it came to the ideas and creativity needed to complete the essay, the student needed very little help. Monica believed that the student could have produced the same quality essay with any other teacher who provided words of encouragement and belief in the student's ability to succeed. How do stereotypes play into this scenario? A kid who is thought, by his peers and teachers, to be a troublemaker incapable of doing any work will eventually internalize these beliefs and become what is expected of him. As teachers, we must move beyond these oppressive stereotypes and ensure all of our students reach their full potential.

An interviewee from Michelle Alexander's (2010) *The New Jim Crow* further explains how self-fulfilling prophecies work in schools:

> *At my school my teachers talk about calling the cops again to take me away.... The cop keeps checking up on me. He's always at the park making sure I don't get into trouble again.... Shit don't change. I just say if you're gonna treat me as a criminal then I'm gonna treat you like I am one, you feel me?* (p. 171)

As evidenced in this excerpt, if we let stereotypes inform our expectations of groups or individuals, there is an increased likelihood that people will internalize these stereotypes and embody them. On the other hand, if we work towards recognizing the stereotypes we hold and begin to critically interrogate and reflect upon the implicit bias embedded in our thoughts and beliefs, we can more accurately form an opinion of people based on who they are and, in the case of youth, who they aspire to be as adults. YPAR is a process that pushes us to move away from stereotypes and provides a path for youth to discover their own power and voice.

## YPAR & Finding Your Voice

"Find your voice" and "use your voice" are strange phrases when you think about it. This notion of finding one's voice might prompt a number of questions. What do you mean find my voice? I have a voice and use it comfortably every day. When will I know if I have actually found my voice? Will it sound different? What does finding your voice look like? It can be confusing to consider what it actually means to find your voice. I'm sure there are seminars and workshops you can attend and books you can read, but truly, it is something you have to mostly figure out on your own. However, the YPAR process is an approach to curriculum, pedagogy and research that can impact the path to finding your voice. As a research method and pedagogical approach, "participatory action research consistently reminds us that any real, lasting positive change in education must derive from the ideas and voices of those living and learning on the ground" (Ayala et al., 2018, p. 8).

When youth engage in YPAR, it gives them the opportunity to identify an issue they see in their school and/or community, research it, and take some kind of collective action. Finding your voice means figuring out what you believe in and standing up for it. YPAR provides a path to better understanding issues of power, privilege, and oppression and, ultimately, developing an action plan that will work towards eradicating the issue you have identified. The passion that burns inside of you to do something—that is your voice. The next step is to use it in the service of equity and justice.

Bursting out often in a scream or shout, our voices are among what makes us, as humans, unique. It gives us the ability to speak for ourselves and not be spoken for. I challenge the notion that children are meant to be seen and not heard. Sitting around and listening to the same commentary year after year from the same old stuffy voices adds nothing new to the conversation. We become complacent in our thoughts. But the voice of a child, the strength that they conjure from daring to speak up, can propel our thoughts in new and exciting directions. The voices of youth can push us to challenge our perspectives and consider fresh, new perspectives. In thinking about the idea of using your voice, we remember the wise words of Audre Lorde (2007):

> *I have come to believe over and over again that what is most important to me must be spoken, made verbal and shared, even at the risk of having it bruised or misunderstood.* (p. 40)

YPAR is a process in which youth can claim their voices and speak back to the deficit narratives and oppressive systems that seek to stifle and silence their voices. Through the YPAR process, we break through the systemic barriers and center the voices of youth. However, while embracing our voices and inner fire, it is also important to recognize that there is more to the equation than just learning how to find and use our voices to express ourselves. It is also imperative that we take action.

I'm not sure which is more difficult, finding our voices or using them. Finding our voices can be a struggle as we grow older and have more experiences. These experiences shape our morals and values, resulting in shaping and changing where we stand on important issues. Our experiences may clash with our long-held beliefs, and then, we have to decide where we stand. More fully understanding our beliefs and values helps to unleash our voices, but then how do we use them? Our voices can be inside of our heads and can fuel our actions silently, but our voices also have the potential to fuel the actions of others. If we hope to impact others and motivate them to take action, our voices must be heard. Voices deserve to be heard. As women in our early twenties, we are still trying to figure out what it means to find our voices. One might assume that we had more clashing experiences, in which our beliefs were challenged, than the youth we were working with, simply because we are twice their age, but that did not seem to be the case. Regardless of their age, our mentors had a grasp on difficult situations way before we personally did in our lives.

The beauty of the YPAR work is that we had the opportunity to grow alongside our mentors. Talking about their experiences brought a new lens to my life, and it added to my personal voice. Our lives and past experiences clashed. But they clashed in a way that created a powerful, collective voice made up of individual voices. In the beginning of this past year, I personally felt angry and defeated. I knew about the oppression in our society, but I did not have conversations about it or dig deeper than the surface. I felt discouraged to find my voice within a society that has not changed its outlook on racism, sexism, etc. I often wonder how other people fail to understand their actions. But I was also telling myself, "I'm just one person, I won't be able to make a difference." I feel like this mentality carried over into our YPAR project with the sixth and seventh graders, but through this process, I've come to believe that our voices do matter, and we can make a difference. bell hooks eloquently expresses the power of finding your voice, especially in the struggle for liberation:

> *Moving from silence into speech is for the oppressed, the colonized, the exploited, and those who stand and struggle side by side a gesture of defiance that heals, that makes new life and new growth possible. It is that act of speech, of "talking back," that is no mere gesture of empty words, that is the expression of our movement from object to subject—the liberated voice.* (p. 9)

It's going to be inspiring to watch our mentors' voices continue to grow. I hope they continue to have experiences that clash and share that clash with others. That is one way they will be able to find strength in their voices. They have helped me find strength in mine, and I'm looking forward to strengthening it more. No matter where they are in their journey in finding their voices, their voices deserve to be heard.

**The Importance of Listening**

Working with the youth through our YPAR project was beneficial to each of us in different ways. For Monica, working with the middle schoolers of Lilyfield helped her to realize that she preferred to work with students in the middle childhood age range, because they still have the spark of curiosity that ignites deeper learning and understanding that she hadn't seen as much in the high school levels of education. Due to this, she changed her major from Adolescent Young Adult English Education to Middle Childhood Education with a specialization in Language Arts and Social Studies. For another student in the group (as previously discussed), the value of finding her voice was key, and for another member of the group, the importance of listening was the biggest take-away. Below she describes the importance of listening.

When I was in elementary school, my father initially taught me this important lesson through the phrase, "you learn more by listening than speaking." While I'd like to think that I have mostly adhered to this, at the beginning of this past school year, September of 2016, I had a helpful reminder. Being a part of the Urban Cohort Program reminds me of that important lesson that I learned long ago from my father. Listening is key. We have to listen to young people and let them know that we hear them. We can do this by supporting and walking alongside them. YPAR provides space for this and creates space for youth to feel valued, heard, and understood.

Through thinking and reflecting upon the YPAR work and its impact on finding voice, I have come to conceptualize three different ways that adults either encourage or stifle the voices of youth. First, there are the adults who tell youth to keep their heads low, their voices hushed, and to focus all of their efforts on listening, simultaneously discouraging any original thought. Unfortunately, we also see this practice in schools, particularly in urban schools. This idea mirrors what Jean Anyon (1980) found in her study of five schools in New Jersey. The teachers in the schools Anyon defined as working class used more direct instruction based on rote learning and what Paulo Freire (1970) calls the "banking model of education" (p. 72). The students in these schools were given little autonomy, thus, hindering their ability to develop higher-order, critical thinking skills. On the other hand, in the more affluent schools, children had more autonomy, were able to work on creative projects, and were prompted to produce knowledge instead of merely consuming it. Second, there are the adults who shock the system to the core and defy complacency at every corner, teaching youth to hold their heads high, value their voices, and not be afraid at any cost. Finally, the rarest group of adults are those individuals who teach youth to stand their ground and to not be afraid of their beliefs, but while using their voices, they simultaneously remind youth of the importance of learning how to actively listen.

In my opinion, the third group is the most beneficial—those who teach students to find their voices, but also to listen. It takes a lot of courage to speak up on behalf of our own beliefs and utilize our voices in a place where it may not seem to matter or make that much of an impact. However, it is an entirely new challenge, which takes bravery and patience, to go into a space and actively listen to the thoughts and feelings expressed, rather than asserting dominance. bell hooks (2000) reminds us that "listening does not simply mean we hear other voices when they speak but we also learn to listen to the voice of our own hearts as well as inner voices" (p. 157). However, this process of actively listening can be difficult, because there is no right amount of time to partake in this, and if you are like me, learning how to sit down and be quiet can take some time to master. Listening and working alongside youth, instead of for them, is a key component of the YPAR process. Having new ideas and bringing them into the conversation is great but only after we have spent time listening and trying to understand and connect more deeply to the needs and desires of the youth we are working alongside. Then comes the second step of finding inner strength and making ourselves heard. It is important to note that this type of engagement is not meant to hinder our voices in the slightest. It is meant to help us come to the realization that we are not the only people in the room with something constructive to say or add. It is important to help youth understand the power of collaboration and community building.

## Concluding Thoughts

We learned a valuable lesson through the YPAR process. For future projects, we will always ground our work in community assets. Focusing on deficits from the start plays right into the neoliberal, capitalist model we were seeking to disrupt. The focus on what was wrong with the community from the start reified deficit narratives that play into oppression. It's important to identify problems, the symptoms that these problems create, and interrogate the root causes so that we can take effective and informed action. We can better do this if we start with the assets in the community at large, as well as the assets within our YPAR collaboratives. Tapping into our collective and individual power is necessary in order to work towards transformative social change. YPAR is a tool that requires this approach. Thus, we have all learned immensely through this process, and we will put these powerful lessons to use in our future classrooms.

# References

Alexander, M. (2016). *The new Jim Crow: Mass incarceration in the age of colorblindness.* New York, NY: New Press.

Anyon, J. (1980). Social class and the hidden curriculum of work. *The Journal of Education, 162*(1), 67-92.

Ayala, J., Cammarota, J., Berta-Ávila, M. I., Rivera, M., Rodríguez, L. F., & Torre, M. E.(2018). *Par entremundos: A pedagogy of the Américas.* New York, NY: Peter Lang.

Cammarota, J., & Fine, M. (2008). *Revolutionizing education: Youth participatory action research in motion.* New York, NY: Routledge.

DiAngelo, R. (2018). *White fragility: Why it's so hard to talk to white people about racism.* Boston, MA: Beacon Press.

Dutton, T. A. (2001). *Violence by any other name.* Cincinnati: The Miami University Center for Community Engagement. Retrieved from https://blogs.miamioh.edu/cce-otr/files/2016/10/VIOLENCE-BY-ANY-OTHER-NAME.pdf

Florence, N. (1998). *bell hooks' engaged pedagogy: A transgressive education for critical consciousness.* West Port, CT: Bergin & Garvey.

Freire, P. (1970). *Pedagogy of the oppressed.* New York, NY: Continuum.

Freire, P. (1998). *Pedagogy of freedom: Ethics, democracy and civic courage.* Lanham, MD: Rowman & Littlefield Publishers.

hooks, b. (1989). *Talking back: Thinking feminist, thinking black.* Boston, MA: South End Press.

hooks, b. (2000). *All about love: New visions.* New York, NY: HarperCollins Inc.

hooks, b. (2002). *Communion: The female search for love.* New York, NY: HarperCollins Inc.

Lorde, A. (2007). The transformation of silence into language and action. In A. Lorde (ed.), *Sister Outsider: Essays and speeches by Audre Lorde* (pp. 40-44). New York, NY: Tenspeed Press.

Mirra, N., Garcia, A., & Morrell, E. (2016). *Doing youth participatory action research: Transforming inquiry with researchers, educators and students.* New York, NY: Routledge.

Morrell, E. (2006). Youth-initiated research as a tool for advocacy and change in urban schools. In S. Ginwright, P. Noguera, & J. Cammarota (Eds.), *Beyond resistance! Youth activism and community change: New democratic possibilities for practice and policy for America's youth* (pp. 111-128). New York, NY: Routledge.

Nieto, S. (2018). Foreword. In J. Ayala, J. Cammarota, M. I. Berta-Ávila, M. Rivera, L. F. Rodríguez, & M. E. Torre (Eds.), *PAR Entremundos: A pedagogy of the Americas* (pp. xv-xvii). New York, NY: Peter Lang Publishing.

Olson, J. D., & Appunn, F. D. (2017). The technology adoption process model and self-efficacy of distance education students [abstract]. *Quarterly Review of Distance Education, 18*(2), 57-76.

Power Inspires Progress (PIP). (2018). *Venice on Vine: Who we are.* Retrieved from http://pip-cincy.com/

Sensoy, O., & Banks, J. A. (2012). *Is everyone really equal? An introduction to key concepts in social justice education.* New York, NY: Teachers College Press.

Solorzano, D. G., & Yosso, T. J. (2001). From racial stereotyping and deficit discourse toward a critical race theory in teacher education. *Multicultural Education, 9*(1), 2-8.

Strobel, K., Osberg, J., & McLaughlin, M. (2006). Participation in social change: Shifting adolescents' developmental pathways. In S. Ginwright, P. Noguera, & J. Cammarota (Eds.), *Beyond resistance! Youth activism and community change: New Democratic possibilities for practice and policy for America's youth* (pp. 197-214). New York, NY: Routledge.

Yosso, T. J. (2005). Whose culture has capital? A critical race theory discussion of community cultural wealth. *Race, Ethnicity and Education, 8*(1), 69-91.

## Interlude

## YPAR Project Introduction: Urban Elementary School

By Janet Albright-Willis, teacher

Abraham Maslow (1976) said, "What is necessary…to change the person…is to change his awareness of himself" (p. 89).

I teach at an urban elementary school where our school slogan is "Where learning is embraced with love." Our school has an enrollment of 409 students. The racial demographics for our school include 92% African American students, 4% multiracial students, 3% Non-White Hispanic students, and 1% white students. We are a school with 98.6% of our students classified as economically disadvantaged. Our school is considered a Community Learning Center, which means that, outside of the academics, we are a hub for various services for our school families. We have a full-time resource coordinator who is responsible for recruiting partnerships with businesses and organizations that will support our students in their learning environment. We have a Parent Center that offers our students' care-takers parenting, job readiness, and GED classes. We also have an in-house, fully operational, health clinic that provides medical services to students, their families, and staff. Our auxiliary health room allows our school to offer dental services on a limited basis to the students and referral services for non-school siblings and caretakers. There is a full-time mental health therapist who provides services to our students.

This urban school is located in an area of the city that has seen many changes over the last five years. Currently, gentrification or redevelopment (depending on one's viewpoint) is occurring at a pace that is affecting our school culture. Families are being relocated to other areas of the city. These moves are sometimes traumatic for the students being displaced from the community they know as home. Peter Kwong (as quoted in Joshi, 2005) said, "Living in this gentrification environment is much more difficult for residents. Actually, what they're doing is killing the indigenous culture" (p. 3).

The partnership between this urban school and Miami University is in its tenth year of growth and continual learning. Students in grades 5 and 6 come together and act as mentors to the Miami University Urban Cohort students in year one of the program. The 5th and 6th grade students talk about concerns related to their school and/or community that they are passionate about and want to take some type of action on. They take this time to educate the Miami Urban Cohort students on concerns surrounding violence, homelessness, their rapidly changing community, education, greenspace for playing, and the lack of good healthy food options available. The student mentors, with the help of the Miami Urban Cohort mentees, began the process of narrowing their concerns down to one or two that they felt strongly about and, through a vote, want to research with the hope of taking some type of action toward the concerns chosen.

This chapter presents discussions from the viewpoints of the Miami Urban Cohort students on the Youth Participatory Action Research conducted with their student mentors around the topic of food insecurity. Both mentors and mentees were charged with the responsibility of working as a cohesive body throughout this YPAR process. What you will see in this chapter are the steps taken within the progression towards their findings and how they applied their findings to action. What I hope you will take away from this chapter is the process of and strength within the YPAR procedure, the "WOW" moments shared by the mentees in their own awakening surrounding this concern within our school community, and a sense of what equitable change we can work on for the betterment of our society.

## References

Joshi, P. (2005). Chinatown seeking a rebirth. *Newsday*, Retrieved from http://www.gmprintingny.com/data/downloads/english_news/Newsday.pdf

Maslow, A. (1976). Religions, values, and peak-experiences. New York, NY: Penguin Books.

# Chapter 5: My Hood is Bad for My Health

By Samantha Thompson, Ash McCartney, Breaysha Helm, Audri Johnson, Joanie Moss, Wil Hughes

During the 2016-2017 academic year, our first year of the Urban Cohort (UC) program, we embarked on a transformative journey alongside fifth and sixth graders of color in a local urban school working on the issue of food insecurity. Through the iterative, dialogic process of engaging in Youth Participatory Action Research (YPAR), these youth moved from discussing the issues of homelessness, violence, bullying, and poverty to the issue of food insecurity in their school neighborhood.

## Our Positionalities

We are all students in the UC program at Miami University. Five out of the six of us are in the department of Teacher Education and will one day have classrooms of our own. The sixth group member is in Speech Pathology and will also likely engage with students in the K-12 setting after graduation. Our time within the UC has already begun to shape us into the transformative educators/practitioners we hope to be alongside our future students, and we are confident our time in the cohort will continue to help us grow into the teachers/practitioners we want to be for our students. In regard to our social locations, five of us identify as white and one of us identifies as Black. Three of us are middle class or above and three of us identify as working class. Engaging in social justice work requires deep, critical introspection. It's important to identify who we are. Our race and social class impact how we navigate and make sense of the world around us. Given that most of us identify as white, we realize that there are things we may struggle to understand in working with students who identify as Black. We have to critically reflect upon our whiteness to try and mitigate the ways in which our white identities may reinforce systems of oppression, even when that is not our intention. Continual self-interrogation compels us to approach the work with humility and a willingness to reside in the uncomfortable and difficult while recognizing the role our whiteness and our implicit connections to colonialism contribute to inequity (DiAngelo, 2011; Sensoy & DiAngelo, 2017).

As first year students in the UC, the six of us had the opportunity to work alongside 13 youth mentors of color from a local school, Urban Elementary, who volunteered to be a part of the YPAR project. Five of the students were male, eight were female, and their teacher was a woman of color.

## YPAR

Inspired by the work of Paulo Freire (1970), YPAR is a powerful tool that is used both as a research methodology and an approach to pedagogy (Foster-Fishman, Law, Lichty, &

Aoun, 2010). YPAR is defined as a process of working with youth to assist them in identifying concerns in their community and taking leadership in influencing policies and decisions that impact them (Ozer & Douglas, 2013). YPAR is grounded in the questions and concerns of the youth who are both participants and leaders within the project. "Youth participation is defined as adolescents partaking in and influencing processes, decisions and activities in the community and in research on the community" (Wattar, Fanous, & Berliner, 2012, p. 187). As a methodology, YPAR delves deeper into how people understand their lives and communities. In an educational setting, it works as a knowledge bridge between the classroom and the realities of students, enabling them to make change based on their lived experiences (Cammarota & Romero, 2011). For researchers interested in social justice and community change, YPAR is a viable option. As a research method, YPAR has been conceptualized as potentially transformative because of the insider knowledge the youth bring to the topic of study (Carabello, Lozenski, Lyiscott, & Morrell, 2017; Ginwright & Cammarota, 2007; Ginwright & James, 2002; Radina et al., 2018; Schwartz, 2006). By engaging in the YPAR process, youth voices are centered in identifying issues, questioning, and critically examining those issues and responding with action (Cammarota & Fine, 2008; Radina et al., 2018). Typically, youth from urban communities have been silenced and have not been given ready access to the means to engage in democratic processes that push for social change. Through YPAR, youth are engaged collaboratively in a process positioning them as the experts, moving from having research done on them to research being done with them. YPAR pushes back against traditional approaches to research, seeking to lessen hierarchical powers that typically exist between youth and adults. Unlike traditional research, YPAR includes those individuals being researched in the process, who also guide the research process. YPAR allows participants to devise questions and collect and interpret data while reflecting on the entire process (Samuelson, Smith, Stevenson, & Ryan, 2013). Researchers engaged in this type of process should work carefully to ensure negative effects of existing social hierarchies positioning researchers as experts and co-researchers as informants are not exacerbated or reinforced (Chabot, Shoveller, Spencer, & Johnson, 2012). YPAR challenges social isolation through a democratic process in which participants engage in self-reflexive evaluation that is collaborative and reciprocal. YPAR is powerful because it "provides young people with opportunities to study social problems affecting their lives and then determine actions to rectify those problems" (Cammarota & Fine, 2008, p. 2).

A key component of the YPAR work is developing deep and meaningful relationships with youth. This means engaging in the process of telling stories, dialoguing, identifying issues/generative themes, deciding on actions, reflecting, and continuing through that cycle. Our YPAR work occurred in two spaces: Urban Elementary and Peaslee Neighborhood Center, a long-standing community center located several blocks from the school. In the following section, we describe the school our youth mentors attended.

## Urban Elementary

Urban Elementary is a public school in a large, midwestern, urban school district that, during the period of the work shared here, served approximately 34,000 students (per the school district's annual report). Upon walking into the school during each of our visits, we observed teachers striving to meet their students where they are. "Preparing students for Life" is displayed on banners throughout the school. The faculty and staff work to have students see the value in education and relationships. The school offers many additional resources and services to their students and families in regard to educational opportunities, extracurricular activities, after school care, counseling, a school-based community health clinic, English as a Second-Language curricula, and summer courses. Urban is one of the district's Community Learning Centers that have community partners/agencies working in the schools to provide these wrap-around services to the youth and their families.

One very special component of the school is the long-standing Parent Resource Center. This space, open during school hours, is staffed by district personnel and, most importantly, long-time parent volunteers. These parents host children throughout the school day who are in need in a variety of ways. Some are sent by a teacher in the building for a "time out" to regroup and, in the words of one of the parent volunteers, "Time to wash your face, baby, and get a new start." Literally, children are invited to wash their faces, get a hug, perhaps have their hair fixed, maybe a set of clean clothes, a bite to eat, etc. What matters to the parents is that the needs of the children have been met and that they are ready to go back to class and learn. The school is situated to serve the whole child by providing services and opportunities in a context of relationship building.

## Urban Elementary Sessions

We, the Miami students, would arrive at Urban Elementary for our Friday sessions at the time school was letting out for the day. Children would be meeting parents outside. Teachers would direct car and pedestrian traffic. Teachers and children and parents would be connecting. Often, Janet, the teacher with whom we worked, was on duty outside at this time. We would make small talk, connect with a few of the students with whom we worked, and then make our way to Janet's class where we prepped materials and sometimes a snack. Upon the arrival of Janet and the youth mentors, there was always time for small talk as we were setting up to get ready during our transition period. During that time, youth mentors related what they had experienced recently: maybe about what happened in a classroom or the cafeteria or what they did the day before after school. The youth asked the Miami students about their own experiences, interests, and their own days, as well. To enter into the YPAR work, it was important to make time for the youth and the Miami students to build community and trust. These conversations, with no agenda other than to listen and hear one another, helped to facilitate this. Early on in the process, Janet also engaged the whole group in trust building and icebreaker activities.

Part of the sessions early on were about engaging with the youth in dialogues about social justice. While the Miami students had been discussing social justice in their first-year seminar, for many of the Urban Elementary youth, it was the first time hearing about this term. To enter the exploration, Janet started a dialogue with the youth:

| |
|---|
| Janet: *Have you heard the words, Social justice? What do you think these words mean?* |
| Together, the words did not mean much. |
| Janet: *Let's separate them. Social. What do you think of when you hear the word 'social'?* |
| Student: *Being with somebody, hanging around somebody.* |
| Janet: *What do you think Justice means?* |
| Student: *Unfair, fair, something that is right.* |
| Janet: *Where do you see these words? Where do you see social?* |
| The students: *Social Studies.* |
| Janet: *Where do you see "justice"?* |
| The students: *The unit on diversity.* [The district has moved to literacy units. One of those units includes diversity, experiencing diversity in one's life. Through the unit, students begin to think about how to overcome adversity and the way this is connected to justice.] |
| Janet: *How do we use these words? So now, what do you think both of them together mean?* |
| Janet asks the students to help her visualize it when they struggle and are still not able to get a clear picture of it. |

After the students dialogue about what social justice is, they move onto trying to identify an issue to further research for their YPAR project.

**Issue Identification**

Youth mentors were asked to identify a pressing social justice issue in their community. As the youth went around the room, they identified homelessness, violence, bullying, and poverty as issues of concern. As these issues were identified, they were written up and placed around the room on separate pieces of chart paper. Once the issues were identified, students were asked to go to the chart paper of the issue about which they felt most strongly. Students formed groups based on topics with the Miami students and then they began to talk about that particular topic and identify areas within that topic. Some of the discussions within the groups involved problems that they saw within that particular topic.

For example, in the poverty group, they discussed the lack of money, hunger, and the daily struggles to meet the needs of people who are living in poverty. Students in the violence group identified symptoms of the issues. In particular, the youth talked about violence and how it included fighting, suicide, shooting, and breaking and entering. They also brainstormed possible actions, including a petition to take away guns and knives, therapy and resources, and neighborhood watch groups. The students working on the bullying issue talked about how verbal bullying can lead to physical violence. They also discussed the prevalence of cyberbullying. Additionally, the students identified plans to stop bullying. One of the biggest takeaways on their chart was developing awareness of bullying and its causes. The students who were working on homelessness discussed a lot of the different factors related to homelessness and, in particular, how the loss of jobs can contribute to homelessness. They concluded that everyone should have a place to live.

Once they completed their chart paper, each group came back to report to the larger group. At that point, the full group listened to each of the four topics that were identified, and then their goal was to narrow it down to just one topic. After a discussion between the youth mentors and college student mentees, they decided that the topic of poverty was the largest umbrella and that homelessness, bullying, and violence fell under the category of poverty. As Janet began to listen to the conversations about poverty, she realized that the students' narratives about what poverty was and what poverty looks like were a little distorted. The youth didn't realize that they were describing situations that they were a part of as if they were not. In order to move forward with the topic of poverty at this point, Janet felt she needed to help her students understand that sometimes our narratives block the truth.

Many of our students felt that poverty was caused by a lack of willingness to work. However, Janet pushed the group, all of them, to consider larger factors that impact one's circumstance of poverty. The students learned that, within the context of their city, the line between living in poverty and not rested on whether or not a family of four made above or below $26,000. Then, the students were asked what costs were associated with the day-to-day living for a family of four. How much does it cost to rent where you live? What about the cost of food for a month? How much is gas and electric for a month? What about the costs for the other basic needs for a month for a family of four? Janet also challenged the students to give her the cost of the shoes they were wearing. How much does clothing cost? What about the video games all of the youth played? What about entertainment outside of the house? They began to deduct those line item costs from the $26,000 with the understanding that falling below $26,000 meant someone was definitely under the poverty line. Once the youth started looking at that magic line and seeing how easy it was, just with daily living expenses, to move above and below that magic line, they began to more clearly understand the concept of poverty.

To further their dialogue and deepen their consciousness, Janet led the students in a musical chairs activity. However, unlike the typical musical chairs, when a chair was removed and the last student had nowhere to sit, the game was over for that student. In this version, the students, Urban and Miami students, had to think about taking on an identity assigned by Janet. Each identity was related to a social justice issue: a person experiencing homelessness, a mother of two who lost housing, not being able to afford medicine, experiencing mental health issues, troubles with transportation, etc. In the end, when the final student was in a chair, Janet indicated that ultimate privileges come with that chair. Janet asked her, "How did it feel to be the last one standing with all the privilege?" Smiling, she said she felt good, that she had "Won!" Students who lost their seats were asked to tell a story about how they found themselves with their particular challenge. Janet wanted these issues to be contextualized. For example, Henry had been assigned the identity of a homeless man who slept under the overpass. The student narrated a story about job loss and not being able to get care for mental health issues. These challenges led to his current experience of homelessness. A Miami student, assigned the homeless mother, said she holds a sign "Homeless with kids, please help" to get money after leaving an abusive relationship. The students, all of them, began to look beyond the individual and blaming the individual and explore the larger societal and systemic contexts that lead to the positions in which some people find themselves.

**Neighborhood Center Sessions**

Saturdays at the Neighborhood Center were similarly structured to sessions at the school. At the start of the session, everyone would be given time to wake up, decompress from their week, and would begin to get comfortable with each other again. As a group, the youth further explored the concept of poverty when they played the online game, *Spent* (Urban Ministries of Durham, 2010), where players take on the role of someone who is in poverty and must live paycheck to paycheck, as well as live through everyday occurrences, such as paying your bills, going to the grocery store, etc. Players also have a child they must take care of, which contributes to how important decisions in the game are made. It was through this game that everyone began to understand what living in poverty looks like on a day-to-day basis. Some of the Miami mentees and the youth mentors had an intimate, lived experience with poverty, but we all still needed a better understanding of the systemic factors that keep poverty in place.

The topic of poverty was further explored and understood as each participant went through simulations depicting how poverty can impact the lives of individual people and how one random occurrence can affect a person's whole life. This activity also illustrated how common issues can intersect to exacerbate the impact of poverty. For example, how mental health can contribute to poverty and create conditions in which it is harder to get necessary medical attention. At that point, the student mentors began to move away from the notion of poverty being due to laziness and immorality and began to see the institutional and systemic issues that create and maintain these circumstances. They saw how varied and individualized poverty can be, even if a majority of a community is experiencing it at the same time.

As the semester progressed, the group as a whole began to move away from the general topic of poverty and decided to focus more on food insecurity and its visible effects on the community. The students wanted to focus specifically on the availability and accessibility of healthy food options in the community. While Janet often times determined the activities used to engage all of us in the topic we discussed on any given day, there were some sessions when the Miami students were responsible for choosing a focus related to food insecurity and creating activities to engage with the topic. Often, we played games, like the one mentioned above, that exposed both Miami students and youth mentors to common situations that people experiencing food insecurity go through. These games and activities raised more questions about these experiences, as well as changed outlooks on the people students and mentors saw on a daily basis who were experiencing food insecurity. There were times when everyone had to step back from the learning and the conversations and look inward to see how their own opinions and biases affected our work on this issue and how we regarded the people around us. These sessions at the neighborhood center never left us satisfied, and we always left with more questions about our topic and the people it involved. The main questions we had during these Saturdays were, "Why does this happen?" and "What do we do?" This is when the research process began to deepen.

**Exploring Food Insecurity**

According to Feeding America (2018), food insecurity and chronic disease is a cycle that begins when the "family cannot afford enough nutritious food" (n.p.). When stress and poor nutrition are combined, more challenges can occur. When these problems start to affect the family financially, that means there is less money to spend on nutritious food and medical care. In addition, if people do not know where their next meal is coming from, that becomes their central focus, which means that they do not have much room to think about anything else.

When families and individuals have to do anything that they can to survive and feed their families, the issue becomes whether or not societal means are put in place for these individuals who cannot afford to feed themselves. Resources are available but vary in accessibility. Food stamps are vouchers given to low income individuals and families to use for food. In order to receive food stamps in Ohio, according to the Ohio Department of Job and Family Services (ODJFS, 2019), a family's income "cannot exceed 130 percent of the federal poverty guidelines" (n.p.). These guidelines, for the year of 2016, state that a family of four must make at or below $24,600 yearly. For SNAP food benefits, the net income of a household is multiplied by 0.3 before being subtracted from the maximum amount possible for a household of that size.

Once a family applies for and start receiving food stamps, they are given a card that resembles a credit or debit card. They are free to use their card anywhere that food stamps are accepted, but it cannot be exchanged for cash, sold to other individuals, or used for illegal activity. Food stamps cannot be used on products such as alcohol and tobacco. In addition, they cannot be used to purchase hot foods, paper products, personal care items, etc. Families receiving food stamps are alerted of these restrictions when they receive their cards. This means that families cannot buy items such as toilet paper, soap, laundry detergent, diapers, or feminine hygiene products with their food stamps. Most large-scale grocery stores and other retailers that sell food products accept food stamps. However, unless the family is also receiving cash benefits on that same card, fast food and other restaurants are typically off limits for food stamp benefits.

In Cincinnati's urban neighborhoods, there are not many grocery stores, so the community often relies on corner stores and markets when they need to purchase food. This is due to the fact that bigger grocery chains with better quality of food choices, such as Kroger, are further away from where people live, as opposed to corner stores, which are closer in proximity. The prices, variety, and quality of food available at corner stores as compared to larger grocery stores varies widely. Since the youth focused on the topic of food insecurity, members of the YPAR group decided it would be a good idea to investigate the different stores that the youth and their families have access to in the community.

For one Saturday session at the neighborhood center, our youth mentors decided that we should visit three grocery stores within their community. During these visits they investigated the prices and variety of foods, as well as the overall layout of each store. The students chose the following three locations for their investigation: (1) a popular corner store; (2) Kroger; and (3) a local farmer's market, which is increasingly becoming corporatized.

When the students went to the corner store, they observed that there were some canned foods that were expired. One student specifically noticed that the items being sold throughout the store were not priced. The students discovered that the customers brought the items they wanted to purchase to the counter, and the cashier would determine a price.

The group had a discussion about how this may make it more difficult for families and individuals to budget their money when shopping at the corner store. Miami mentees and the youth then traveled to the local Kroger. This Kroger looked like any other grocery store to the students, except for the layout of the entrance. As soon as they entered the store, they took note that non-nutritious food lined the shelves immediately inside the front door and along the first aisle. In many other grocery stores that the mentees had been in, the produce was one of the first things you saw upon entry. The trip came to a conclusion at the historic city market located in the community, and each member discovered that the Market was more of a place to get prepared dishes and specialty items, rather than produce and individual ingredients used to make meals. The students also noticed that the prices at the farmer's market were vastly more expensive than those at the corner stores and Kroger.

In order to continue learning about food insecurity in the neighborhood, the youth mentors created a simple food map that consisted of the students charting the places they visited on a map of the neighborhood, as well as where they used to live in the neighborhood. It was somewhat difficult for the mentees to connect to this particular activity because none of them were still living in the community, so they felt particularly distanced from this specific issue. Through the process of researching food insecurity, a couple of additional discoveries were made by the group.

This activity prompted the group to talk about not only the changes in grocery stores, but in the new stores and restaurants that are appearing in their neighborhood and replacing community businesses. This led to a discussion about the removal of a nearby Kroger and the new Kroger that was built in a more affluent area of town. The youth mentors also brought pictures from when they visited their Kroger location and pictures of the new one in order to help the students see the differences in prices and overall layout of each of these stores. For example, while their neighborhood Kroger was very simple in its layout and had the basic aspects of a grocery store, the new Kroger was multi-floored and had a social aspect that many other groceries do not have. It had many sections of different types of food, as well as a restaurant and a wine tasting and social area. The differences between the two stores helped to illuminate the inequities in regard to the two grocery stores. The one located in the lower income neighborhood was a much lower quality grocery store than the one located in the more affluent area, located near a university. The students found that there were other disparities in their local neighborhood that contributed to food insecurity as well.

Due to gentrification, many of the restaurants and other local businesses have price points that the students and their families cannot afford. One of the few affordable establishments, a local pizza place, is a pizzeria and community catering business. It is frequented by the community and is an invaluable resource in the community. Unlike the pizza place, many of the restaurants are not affordable. The group also did some research on what these new restaurants and bars were selling and what was actually being charged. Here there is a chart depicting some of the information they found:

| (Restaurant names have been replaced with pseudonyms) | Average Price | Most Expensive Item |
| --- | --- | --- |
| Banton Kitchen | • Breakfast: $6.30<br>• Lunch:$7.80<br>• Drinks: $3.30<br>• Sides:$2.64 | • Breakfast:$11<br>• Lunch:$10<br>• Drink:$5<br>• Side: $3 |
| Churi | • Breakfast:$12.10<br>• Lunch/Dinner: $9.13<br>• Drinks:$9.40 | • Breakfast:$15<br>• Lunch/Dinner:$15<br>• Drinks:$10 |
| Sweet Barbeque | • Lunch/Dinner:$13.80<br>• Sides:$2.25<br>• Drinks:$1.58 | • Lunch/Dinner:$30<br>• Sides:$2.25<br>• Drinks:$2.25 |
| Johnny's Pizzeria | • Lunch/Dinner:$14.12<br>• Sides:$5.51<br>• Salads:$2.95<br>• Desserts:$2.75 | • Lunch/Dinner:$25.62<br>• Sides:$10.45<br>• Salads:$2.95<br>• Desserts:$2.75 |
| Playa | • Appetizers:$7.30<br>• Soups/Salads:$8.75<br>• Lunch/Dinner:$13.23<br>• Sides:$4 | • Appetizers:$12<br>• Soups/Salads:$10<br>• Lunch/Dinner:$39<br>• Sides:$6 |
| Pizza Palace | • Appetizers:$5.95<br>• Pizzas:$17.54<br>• Sandwiches:$7.45<br>• Beverages:$2<br>• Desserts:$4<br>• Salads:$6.12 | • Appetizers:$5.95<br>• Pizzas:$18<br>• Sandwiches:$7.95<br>• Beverages:$2<br>• Desserts:$5<br>• Salads:$6.95 |
| Signature Pub | • Lunch/Dinner:$6.38<br>• Brunch:$6.83 | • Lunch/Dinner:$8.75<br>• Brunch:$7.50 |

Through our research, it became clear that gentrification was contributing to food insecurity in the neighborhood, and a lack of access to food is another means of pushing people out of the community. As referenced in the Urban Cohort and Context chapter, gentrification has been occurring at breakneck speed without regard for long-time residents. During the time in which this work was occurring, one of the Miami faculty members was asked if the Urban Elementary students could take on a project-based learning activity for the local business community by creating ideas for a boutique grocery store. Clearly, those pushing gentrification, the local "Renaissance," have no idea the impact of their actions. Despite this kind of egregious ignorance, we decided to look for ways that the community and city at large were trying to combat food insecurity.

We discovered that the Social Enterprise Alliance (S.E.A.) is coming to Cincinnati in the near future. S.E.A. is a company that produces food in big cities by building self-sufficient, solar powered greenhouses for food production. These greenhouses are designed to reduce waste, minimize carbon emissions, and create jobs, while still preserving resources. Their goal is to help provide food and fight malnutrition in bigger cities that are experiencing issues with poverty. The addition of companies like S.E.A. suggests that the city is trying to come up with creative solutions to address food insecurity; however, it would seem that ensuring all communities have access to grocery stores with quality food and competitive pricing would be top priority. We also found that the schools are often utilized as places where families and children have access to food.

One member of our team visited four different local schools to research how the meals were prepared and what was being offered to kids who attended. The four elementary schools in two counties that our team member visited said they provide meals to children and their families who are facing food insecurity. When asked about the qualifications of those who receive these benefits, it was stated that it was those who were identified as "low income" who qualified for food. The schools also provide free meals during the summer months with limitations. If the kids are in summer programs, they are guaranteed a meal; however, not all kids attend these programs year-round. Additionally, leftover food is given to families throughout the week. Although schools can mitigate the impacts of food insecurity, there are perhaps other solutions that would get to the root cause of the problem. Through this process, we learned that food insecurity is a big problem that impacted many of the youth with whom we worked on the project. Our actions involved getting out into the community to get a better understanding of this issue on the local level. We focused more heavily on better understanding the issue because it is a very complex issue and taking action without more fully understanding the issue would have been irresponsible. The process of researching the issue and getting out into the community with the youth was a meaningful, but slow, process. We were working with 5th and 6th grade students and felt it was important to approach the project as a process of understanding and leadership development, as opposed to merely rushing in to take action and address the problem.

Through this project, we also realized the necessary messiness of YPAR, and we learned that it is not race but a marathon. Social change doesn't happen overnight, and the time we spent on the project was meaningful and transformative despite not directly addressing the problem. If there were easy solutions to systemic problems like food insecurity, then there would be no need for projects like this one. These things take time, and this was certainly a lesson in understanding that engaging in the struggle for equity and justice is a lifelong process and a meaningful one.

# References

Cammarota, J., & Fine, M. (2008). *Revolutionizing education: Youth participatory action research in motion*. New York, NY: Routledge.

Cammarota, J., & Romero, A. (2011). Participatory action research for high school students: Transforming, policy, practice, and the personal with social justice education. *Educational Policy, 25*(3), 488-506.

Carabello, L., Lozenski, B. D., Lyiscott, J. J., & Morrell, E. ( 2017). YPAR and critical epistemologies: Rethinking education research. *Review of Research in Education, 41,* 311-336.

Chabot, C., Shoveller, J. A., Spencer, G., & Johnson, J. L. (2012). Ethical and epistemological insights: A case study of participatory action research with young people. *Journal of Empirical Research on Human Research Ethics, 7*(2), 20-33.

DiAngelo, R. (2011). White fragility. *International Journal of Critical Pedagogy, 3*(3), 54-70.

Feeding America. (2018). *Hunger and health.* Rerieved from https://www.feedingamerica.org/research/hunger-and-health-research

Foster-Fishman, P., Law, K., Lichty, L., & Aoun, C. (2010). Youth reACT for social change: A method for youth participatory action research. *American Journal of Community Psychology, 46*(1/2), 67-83.

Freire, P. (1970). *Pedagogy of the oppressed.* New York, NY: Continuum.

Ginwright, S., & Cammarota, J. (2007). Youth activism in the urban community: Learning critical civic praxis within community organizations. *International Journal of Qualitative Studies in Education, 20*(6), 693-710.

Ginwright, S., & James. T. (2002). From assets to agents of change: Social justice, organizing, and youth development. *New Directions for youth development, 96,* 27-46.

Ohio Department of Job and Family Services (ODJFS). (2019). *Our services.* Retrieved from http://jfs.ohio.gov/ocomm_root/1000ourservices.stm

Ozer, E. J., & Douglas, L. (2013). The impact of participatory research on urban teens: An experimental evaluation. *American Journal of Community Psychology, 51,* 66–75.

Radina, R., Schwartz, T., Ross, G., Aronson, B., Albright-Willis, J., Wallace, M., & Norval, B. (2018). A space for us too: Using youth participatory action research to center youth voices. *School-University-Community Partnerships, 11*(4), 122-139.

Samuelson, B. L., Smith, R. T., Stevenson, E., & Ryan, C. (2013). A case study of youth participatory evaluation in co-curricular service learning. *Journal of the Scholarship of Teaching and Learning, 13*(3), 63-81.

Schwartz, T. (2004). Writing and neighborhood voices: "It depends on where you grow up at." *Voices from the Middle, 12*(1), 16-22.

Sensoy, O., & DiAngelo, R. (2017). *Is everyone really equal?: An introduction to key concepts in social justice education.* New York, NY: Teachers College Press.

Urban Ministries of Durham. (2010). *Spent* [Online game]. Retrieved from http://playspent.org/html/

Wattar, L., Fanous, S., & Berliner, P. (2012). Challenges of youth participation in participatory action research: Methodological considerations of the Paamiut Youth Voice research project. *International Journal of Action Research, 8*(2):185-212.

# Chapter 6: Transformation Through Radical Love

By Rachel Radina & Tammy Schwartz

*Whatever I know I know with my entire self; with my critical mind but also
with my feelings, with my intuitions, with my emotions.*
Paulo Freire (2005, p. 54)

The program beautifully connects the community, the university, and the school, grounded in a spirit of activism and resistance to the status quo. It is a space of radical resistance that brings together many wonderful people with hopes and dreams for a future that is more just and equitable. There is a deep sense of radical love within our built, beloved community, and each year we bring new students into the fold. The people engaged in this work are moved and transformed in ways that would not be possible without the support and love of everyone within this sacred circle of trust, comradery, and radical acceptance. Growth is often painful, but necessary. "What a painful, yet beautiful, process it is to become someone" (Radina, 2018, p. 53). We support one another within our own journeys of personal growth and push one another to move beyond what we imagine is possible. As stated by Robin Kelley (2002) "the map to a new world is in the imagination" (p. 2). We look for a vision of change, and we do it in community with one another. This is powerful work that fills the soul. Yet, it is not without challenges and struggles. Doing this type of work requires the ability to lovingly self-critique and challenge one another to move outside of our comfort zones. We can never stop engaging in praxis—we continue to grow through a process of action and reflection (Freire, 1970). bell hooks (2002) calls us back to love, "we need to return to love and proclaim its transformative power" (p. 15), remembering that education that is grounded in the concept of radical love requires personal transformation.

We realize this transformation is a process, and "Sometimes, we fail to realize that students are in the process of becoming, but we also forget that so are we. We need to hold each other accountable but from a place of love and compassion" (Radina, 2018, p. 57). We can't do this work without learning how to love ourselves and one another and we must engage in this act of loving with a fierce urgency because "in dominator culture the killing off of imagination serves as a way to repress and contain everyone within the limits of the status quo" (hooks, 2010, p. 60). When we engage in critical pedagogy, we move away from the repressive forms of education that seek to stifle and suffocate our ability to live and love together and to imagine a world that does not yet exist. We must work "to see the future in the present" and tap into the "revolutionary ideas" of "freedom and love" (Kelley, 2002, pp. 9 & 11). Freedom and love are powerful tools; therefore, we need to move towards the will and freedom to act, keeping in mind that "freedom is acquired by conquest, not by gift" (Freire, 1970, p. 47). Our fight for freedom must always stem from a deep place of radical love—a love that emerges in response to the woundedness inside of us and the woundedness of the world. We must keep in mind that "liberation is thus a childbirth, and a painful one" (Freire, 1970, p. 49). Healing starts with the self and radiates outward. In the first chapter of her book *The Next Great American Revolution*, Grace Lee Boggs (2012) makes the case for a much needed and radical transformation in the way we live our lives, the way in which we conceive and live in communities, and the ways in which government, education, economics, health care, etc., will be reimagined because of that transformation. Our current times, she writes, "are the times to grow our souls" (p. 28). Corporate globalization, education to incarceration, colonization to gentrification to excavation to eradication—out of these dominant cultural forces, she claims, has come the destruction of community. Because of this, *we* now live in places aching for the imbued nuances of deep connectedness with ourselves, others, and the physical spaces we share. How do we move from such isolating forces to wholeness? Most importantly, *what* do we do next to get there? Boggs argues that the answer involves a "new postindustrial world based on partnership among ourselves" (p. 43). For this to happen:

> *Each of us needs to undergo a tremendous philosophical and spiritual transformation. Each of us needs to be awakened to a personal and compassionate recognition of the inseparable interconnection between our minds, hearts, and bodies; between our physical and psychical well-being; and between ourselves and all the other selves in our country and in the world.* (pp. 33-34)

We cannot work towards the transformation that is needed without engaging in a different approach to education and community building.

Baszile (2017) calls for a centering of "justice, love, community and well-being" and to engage with the concept of movement building as part of our work as social justice educators (p. 208). This is important to keep in mind as Angela Davis (2016) reminds us that mass movements are the only thing that has ever brought about change in our society. This requires the embodiment of a radical orientation to love that we bring into all of our relationships—a deep, radical love that reaches the roots, nourishing the soil and allowing for growth that extends beyond our current ways of being and knowing that are currently twisted up and mutilated within systems of oppression. This love is not the soft, sweet love of fairy tales and not something that should be trivialized and deemed unnecessary. There is no way forward within this oppressive, capitalist system without a radical orientation to love that cannot be easily broken, pushed aside, or commodified. Audre Lorde (2007) powerfully stated that "the master's tools can never dismantle the master's house" (p. 112), and we must take these wise words seriously if we hope to tap into transformative change within ourselves and within our communities. We don't get there by merely acquiescing to the current system and the conditions thrust upon us. We get there through solidarity, long-term commitment to struggle, critical self-reflection, and the will to take action, even when we put ourselves at risk, realizing that "propagating a world of radical self-love is both a practice of individual transformation and a commitment to collective transformation" (Taylor, 2018, p. 86). This is what a radical orientation to love requires. We must make a commitment to push for change in all the spaces we find ourselves, this includes higher education.

In his book, *Earth in Mind: On Education, Environment and the Human Prospect*, David Orr (2004) argues for an education focused on ecological design intelligence "motivated by an ethical view of our world and our obligations to it [for]...healthy, durable, resilient, just and prosperous communities" (p. 3). In particular, he sees the current path of higher education as contributing to ecological demise, in part, because of its focus on the head with no attention to the heart. He goes on to claim,

> *the planet does not need more successful people. But it does desperately need more peacemakers, healers, restorers, storytellers, and lovers of every kind. It needs people who live well in their places. It needs people of moral courage willing to join the fight to make the world habitable and humane.* (p. 12)

Engaging in education as the practice of freedom through the use of critical pedagogy is a move to tap into Orr's ideas of what is needed. Paulo Freire's powerful approach to pedagogy was grounded in the idea of love, but love as an action. As stated by Darder (2002) who so eloquently writes about Freire's pedagogy,

> *It was through such love he surmised, that teachers could find the strength, faith, and humility to establish solidarity and struggle together to transform the oppressive ideologies and practices of public education.* (pp. 91-92)

Critical pedagogy is an approach to education that requires educators to work with and alongside their students, instead of merely dictating what it means to know and whose knowledge counts. Critical pedagogy is an approach that counters the "banking model of education," an approach that Freire continued to critique throughout his work. Freire (1970) suggested that "education is suffering from narration sickness" (p. 57), and the banking approach to education firmly keeps the status quo intact and does not allow nor require students to question knowledge or to see themselves as coming into the classroom with knowledge. Through this banking approach to education, "knowledge is a gift bestowed by those who consider themselves knowledgeable upon those they consider to know nothing" (p. 72). Freire firmly believed that true thinking and education can only happen through communication, and thus, "liberation is a praxis: the action and reflection of men and women upon their world in order to transform it" (p. 79). Critical pedagogy, or what Freire often referred to as "problem-posing education," requires students to become "critical co-investigators in dialogue with their teacher" (p. 81).

Michael Dantley (2018) uses the work of Paulo Freire to call for an approach to education that works in the service of justice:

> *Education never could but now most definitely cannot, confine its responsibilities to reading, writing and arithmetic but must locate these within a societal context that demonstrates how these academic skills can have a significant impact on helping to transform the heinous conditions running rampant in society.* (p. 178)

We engage in a transformative approach to education with our students and with the youth who participate in the YPAR program through the use of critical pedagogy. This approach to education transforms students into critical thinkers who see themselves as actors who can make change in their world, as opposed to people who are acted on (Dantley, 2018). This allows students to see how they are both shaped and shape the contexts of their lives.

## Challenges/Limitations

Just as we are in the process of becoming, so is our YPAR work. The work is never finished, and there is always room for growth and to develop a deeper consciousness about the world around us. In a conversation with Myles Horton, Paulo Freire suggests:

> *We are not complete. We have to become inserted in a permanent process of searching. Without this we would die in life. It means that keeping curiosity is absolutely indispensable for us to continue to be or to become.* (Horton & Freire, 1990, p. 11)

YPAR is a messy, non-linear process that takes time and commitment, but we continue to learn and grow both as individuals and as a collaborative community through this process. In a sense, our individual and collective growth models what we hope youth gain through this experience. We have learned through much trial and error that we need to focus on the process of the work, as opposed to the products we might hope to produce. Cannella (2008) suggests that we cannot predict what students will learn through the YPAR process and that "the impact on students is not easily quantifiable" (p. 207). Instead, "PAR as a pedagogy acknowledges that rich learning...requires a long-term investment" (p. 207). It's not that outputs are never important and don't hold value. If we do the work, eventually the fruits of our labor will reveal themselves, yet we may never see these outcomes firsthand. Furthermore, just like grassroots community organizing, the change you get may not be the change you were originally seeking (Davis, 2006). YPAR is context specific, is not a predetermined process, and impacts everyone involved differently. Kelley (2002) pointed out that "social movements generate new knowledge, new theories, new questions" (p. 8). YPAR is similar in that regard, and that is exactly what contributes to the non-linear process. As witnessed in the previous chapters, we see examples of projects starting with one issue, and because of dialogue and reflection (praxis), those topics evolve. For example, the Urban Elementary students began with an array of issues underneath the umbrella of poverty and then narrowed it down to the specific issue of food insecurity. The process of landing on and understanding a complex issue like food insecurity is a long process and one that cannot be rushed. However, along the way, the intent is that students will begin to see themselves as researchers, as leaders, and change-makers in their communities.

The work we are engaged in is also logistically challenging. Our university is relatively far away from our partner schools. It is difficult to get already overcommitted college students to agree to travel 45 minutes to an hour away from campus to do work in a school and/or community that is not their own. It's not that they are not interested or committed, but given the extra travel time, it is a big commitment. However, despite this reality, we have many students involved and dedicated to this work, all of whom are willing to travel to engage in this work. In addition, transporting students to our four partner schools and/or the community center where we often meet requires a great deal of university resources. We have to rent vehicles to transport the students to our partner schools, and this costs our program time and money. In the past, our university had a motor pool, and this made traveling from the university to our partner schools and agencies much easier. Since losing the motor pool due to budget cuts, we have had to both seek out and allocate more resources for transportation than were needed in the past. During this particular year, students were traveling to their partner schools twice a semester and one Saturday a month to the community center where we do the bulk of our work. The distance also limits the number of times we can visit our partner schools and the community center. Transporting the youth mentors from our four partner schools to the community center was also challenging and was mainly left up to their teachers. We have since resolved this issue by going back to meeting in the schools on two Fridays a month. Through this work, we have realized that, in order to make these efforts more sustainable and impactful, we need to engage with the issues identified by the youth for more than one academic year.

Ideally, we would like to keep the YPAR youth engaged in this work as they move through school. At one time, we allocated additional resources for this purpose by having Janet, one of our partner teachers, meet with the youth once they left Urban Elementary and moved on to high school. The youth were spread across multiple high schools in the district in many neighborhoods. Transportation and communication proved difficult. We would like to refine our efforts to find other ways to keep youth engaged longer. In part, we want to honor and deepen our relationships with the youth, should they choose, and exploring issues across multiple years can provide the opportunity for further dialogue, action, and reflection. In addition, many of our Urban Cohort students express a strong desire to continue the work beyond their first year in the program. While we do not require it, some take it upon themselves to continue to make the Friday sessions with the new, incoming first year students in the Cohort. We want to continue to streamline this process so that we have a structure that allows more of the youth and the college students to continue this work after the first year.

Another challenge of the Urban Cohort program is the need to be mindful in regard to our various positionalities. When people engage in this type of work, there is always a need for critical self-reflection, this is especially true for white people. This is also true for folks who may be coming into this work from financially privileged backgrounds. As with any community work that is rooted in social justice, there are challenges that arise in regard to identity and culture. In our own context, we particularly need to be mindful of how issues around race and social class manifest. Many (though not all) of our Urban Cohort students are white, and the majority come from middle to upper class backgrounds, while most of our youth mentors are students of color, mostly Black, and attend schools in high poverty areas. The poverty in their communities is caused by systemic factors (e.g. lack of jobs that pay a living wage, lack of affordable housing, etc.) and is not based on individual or family deficits. Further, the poverty is not fully pervasive; there are also middle-class families within the schools where we work. Although our program is housed in a predominately white institution, we have begun to attract more students of color into the Urban Cohort Program, and as the department of teacher education within our university works to create a pipeline for students of color to become teachers and return to their communities to teach, we expect that trend to continue.

Audre Lorde (2007) illuminated the importance of building community and the recognition of difference within community:

> *Without community there is no liberation, only the most vulnerable and temporary armistice between an individual and her oppression. But community must not mean a shedding of our differences, nor the pathetic pretense that these differences do not exist.* (p. 112)

In doing this work, we have to educate ourselves and our students in regard to different aspects of diversity and identity (not merely race and ethnicity), as well as systems of power, privilege, and oppression. Kelley, Tuck, and Wang (2014) suggest that, in order to build a community grounded in radical empathy, we must work "across identity lines by making them hyper-visible in order to recognize specific struggles that people on different sides of those lines experience" (p. 94). We need a critical approach to education that exposes how our differences impact the way we navigate and experience the world. Hooks (2003) suggests:

*To build community requires vigilant awareness of the work we must continually do to undermine all the socialization that leads us to behave in ways that perpetuate domination.* (p. 36)

Becoming critically conscious is a way of being in the world that helps to deepen and broaden our lenses of analysis and critique. But, hooks (2003) urges that we cannot merely read and learn about white supremacy and racism; we must also use these theories as lenses to better understand and interrogate how systems of power and privilege show up in our own lives. This is work that happens throughout the program, but we realize that this work is always incomplete and never finished. Understanding concepts such as race, ethnicity, social class, gender, ability, and sexuality is not a one-time class discussion or semester long endeavor that, once completed, can be checked off the list of becoming critically conscious. Understanding diversity and systems of power is a life-long process, and so students, as well as faculty, staff, and community partners must be willing to engage in this process for the long haul (Lindsey, Nuri Robbins, & Terrell, 2009; Sensoy & DiAngelo, 2017). As soon as we think we "get it," that is when we can do the most harm, especially as white people. As stated by DiAngelo (2018), "White people find it very difficult to think about whiteness as a specific state of being that could have an impact on one's life and perceptions" (p. 25). This is why it is important that, as white people, we continually do the work of understanding how whiteness impacts our lives and the lives of people of color and "never consider ourselves finished with our learning" (DiAngelo, 2018, p. 153). We must also all continue to learn about racism and the ways it manifests in society and in our own daily practices. Because institutional racism is embedded in all of our institutions due to the history of race and racism in the United States, racism is also present in the structures of the schools where the youth are seeking to push for change.

As discussed in a previous chapter, the high school youth who participated in the YPAR work did not get support from other teachers at their school. It hindered their work and also made them feel unheard. Similar to other scholars who have engaged in this work (e.g. Ayala et al., 2018; Rodríguez, 2018; Irizarry & Brown, 2014), we found there is often a mismatch between the way K-12 schools are set-up and the guiding and transformative principles of YPAR. White supremacy governs all of our institutions (Sensoy & DiAngelo, 2017), and schools are a place where students of color are faced with the choice to either assimilate and leave important pieces of who they are at the classroom door (Fordham, Tuck, & Dimitriadis, 2014) or resist and eventually be pushed out of the school, possibly into the criminal justice system (Morris, 2016; Nocella, Parmar, & Stovall, 2014). YPAR acts as a third space or option, one in which students are seen as powerful knowledge producers and change agents. When teachers engage in this work alongside youth and when young college students come to work in solidarity with them, we push back against the deficit narratives that confine and marginalize. At the same time, those forces at play that necessitate a process such as YPAR do not disappear when we begin this work in those spaces. Therefore, the youth and their teachers are often met with resistance, sometimes so stifling that projects are slowed, put on hold, and sometimes even shut down. This is why it's even more important to have community and university partners that can work alongside youth and their teachers to make space for education that is more liberating and just (see Mirra, Garcia & Morrell, 2016; Radina et al., 2018).

**Strengths of the Work/Growth**

In doing this work, youth begin to see themselves as people who hold power and have the ability to make change in their communities and schools. YPAR taps into "the civic purpose of public education and the idea that schools have a role in preparing young people to become citizens and to contribute to the creation of an ever more just democratic society" (Mirra, Garica, & Morrell, 2016, p. 4). Part of the powerful potential of YPAR is that it provides pedagogical tools that help students become critically conscious and compels them to take action. This is of the utmost importance in urban schools where much of the curriculum is focused on test prep and rote memorization (Milner, 2010), which is a dehumanizing approach to education. "If schools are to become spaces for critical consciousness raising and liberation for marginalized youth, the pedagogical practices of educators must become more humanizing" (Irizarry & Brown 2014, p. 73). We have seen this realized through our YPAR work. Through the YPAR program, we have been able to bring this curriculum into classrooms and to support our collaborating teachers in infusing these methods into their curriculum. In addition, we are preparing future teachers to engage with this type of curriculum and pedagogy in their future classrooms. We want our teacher candidates to co-create curriculum with youth that is centered on youth-identified issues where youth get to enact their agency in the world. Grace Lee Boggs (2012) writes about reimagined educational spaces:

> *Just imagine what our neighborhoods would be like if, instead of keeping our children isolated in classrooms for twelve years and more, we engaged them in community-building activities with the same audacity with which the civil rights movement engaged them in desegregation activities fifty years ago.* (p. 158)

Because we had the opportunity to work with two of our program graduates who now have classrooms of their own, we get to witness firsthand how they incorporate the tenets of YPAR and engage youth in the justice issues of our times. It's very powerful to engage with youth and future teachers in this way, and it has the power to enhance the lives of teachers and their students. Irizarry and Brown (2014) suggest that "teachers and students...should be natural allies in the struggle for educational equity and social justice" (p. 74). We know this to be the case and understand the power of YPAR to create space for collective struggle and school transformation. However, this is not an overnight transformation.

When doing work specifically focused on equity and justice, it's important to keep in mind that change takes time (Noguera, Tuck, & Wayne, 2014). We plant seeds and tend to the soil, but we may not see the change we are working towards. However, through this process, youth come to see themselves differently and realize the power they've had all along (Ayala, et al., 2018; Cammarota & Fine, 2008; Mirra et al., 2016 ; Radina et al., 2018). There is already a fire burning inside of youth. They are full of passion and knowledge. We merely fan the flames. We have faith that "the seeds of resistance sowed into the soil with love, and hope for the future will be the freedom fighters who emerge tomorrow" (Radina, 2018, p. 57). Our hope is that, through the YPAR process, we can help youth tap into "a pedagogy of transformational resistance" that provides a set of tools to push back against the oppressive social conditions that are ever present in the current economic, social and political climate (Cammarota, 2017, p. 189). As stated by Cammarota (2017),

> *Although student organizing may or may not lead to critical transformation, the most important aspect of transformational resistance is 'acknowledging' that systems and institutions can be changed to achieve greater social equity. This acknowledgement emerges from a desire to strive for social justice.* (p. 194)

Resistance is a powerful tool that, when wielded in just the right way, has the power to bring about unimaginable social change (Noguera, Tuck, & Wayne, 2014). This is evidenced in the many mass movements that have led to changes that fell outside of what many folks believed was truly possible. But for those of us who resist, we know in our hearts that the change we fight for so vigorously *is* possible. We have not been tricked into believing that our efforts will remain fruitless. We see the seeds of our resistance blossoming into a beautiful bounty that will feed our souls and transform our society. We feel the possibility of change in our bones, and we embody resistance in every step we take both individually and collectively. We know the power that lies within us, and we will continue to tap this well of resistance as long as we are walking this earth, and thereafter, through the imaginations and actions of youth who inevitably make a different future possible. Transformation through the embodiment of radical love is possible, and YPAR is a research methodology and pedagogy that puts this powerful approach to social change into motion.

# References

Ayala, J., Cammarota, J., Berta-Ávila, M. I., Rivera, M., Rodríguez, L. F., & Torre, M. E. (2018). *Par entremundos: A pedagogy of the Américas.* New York, NY: Peter Lang.

Baszile, D. T. (2017). In pursuit of the revolutionary-not-yet: Some thoughts on education work, movement building, and praxis. *Educational Studies, 53*(3), 206-215.

Boggs, G. L. (2012). *The next American revolution: Sustainable activism for the twenty-first century.* Berkeley, CA: University of California Press.

Cammarota, J. (2017). Youth participatory action research: A pedagogy of transformational resistance for critical youth studies. *Journal for Critical Education Policy Studies, 15*(2), 188-213.

Cammarota, J., & Fine, M. (2008). *Revolutionizing education: Youth participatory action research in motion.* New York, NY: Routledge.

Cannella, C. M. (2008). Faith in process, faith in people: Confronting policies of social disinvestment with PAR as pedagogy for expansion. In J. Cammarota & M. Fine (Eds.), *Revolutionizing education: Youth participatory action research in motion* (pp. 189-212). New York, NY: Routledge.

Dantley, M. (2018). Critical consciousness and spirituality: Deconstructing the colonizing practices of U.S. education through the lens of Paulo Freire and critical spirituality. In P. McLaren & S. Soohoo (Eds.), *Radical imagine-nation: Public pedagogy & praxis* (pp. 177-186). New York, NY: Peter Lang.

Darder, A. (2002). *Reinventing Paulo Freire: A pedagogy of love.* Boulder, CO: Westview Press.

Davis, A. (2006, October 10). *How does change happen?* [Video lecture]. Davis, CA: The Women's Resource Center at UC Davis. Retrieved from https://www.youtube.com/watch?v=Pc6RHtEbiOA

Davis, A. (2016). *Freedom is a constant struggle. Ferguson, Palestine, and the foundations of a movement.* Chicago, IL: Haymarket Books

DiAngelo, R. (2018). *White fragility. Why it's so hard for white people to talk about racism.* Boston, MA: Beacon Press.

Fordham, S., Tuck, E., & Dimitriadis, G. (2014). What does an umbrella do for the rain? On the efficacy and limitations of resistance. In E. Tuck & K. W. Yang (Eds.), *Youth resistance research and theories of change* (pp. 97-106). New York, NY: Routledge.

Freire, P. (1970). *Pedagogy of the oppressed.* New York, NY: Continuum.

Freire, P. (2005). *Teachers as cultural workers: Letters to those who dare teach.* Bouder, CO: Westview Press.

hooks, b. (2002). *Communion: The female search for love.* New York, NY: William Morrow.

hooks, b. (2003). *Teaching community: A pedagogy of hope.* New York, NY: Routledge.

hooks, b. (2010). Teaching critical thinking: Practical wisdom. New York, NY: Routledge.

Horton, M., & Freire, P. (1990). *We make the road by walking*. Philadelphia, PA: Temple University Press.

Irizarry, J. G., & Brown, T. M. (2014). Humanizing research in dehumanizing spaces: The challenges and opportunities of conducting participatory action research with youth in schools. In D. Paris & M. Winn (Eds.), *Humanizing research: Decolonizing qualitative inquiry with youth and communities* (pp. 63-80). Thousand Oaks, CA: Sage Publications.

Kelley, R. D. G. (2002). *Freedom dreams: The black radical imagination*. Boston, MA: Beacon Press.

Kelley, R. D. G., Tuck, E., & Yang, K. W. (2014). Resistance as revelatory. In E. Tuck & K. W. Yang (Eds.), *Youth resistance research and theories of change* (pp. 82-96). New York, NY: Routledge.

Lindsey, R. B., Nuri Robbins, K. & Terrell, R. D. (2009). *Cultural proficiency: A manual for school leaders*. Thousand Oaks, CA: Sage.

Lorde, A. (2007). The master's tools will never dismantle the master's house. In A. Lorde (ed.), *Sister outsider: Essays and speeches by Audre Lorde* (pp. 110-113). New York, NY: Tenspeed Press.

Milner, H. R., IV. (2010). *Understanding diversity, opportunity gaps, and teaching in today's classrooms. Start where you are but don't stay there*. Cambridge, MA: Harvard Education Press.

Mirra, N., Garcia, A., & Morrell, E. (2016). *Doing youth participatory action research: Transforming inquiry with researchers, educators and students*. New York, NY: Routledge.

Morris, M. W. (2016). *Pushout: The criminalization of black girls in schools*. New York, NY: The New Press.

Nocella, A. J., Parmar, P., & Stovall, D. (2014). *From education to incarceration: Dismantling the school-to-prison pipeline*. New York, NY: Peter Lang.

Noguera, P., Tuck, E., & Yang, W. (2014). Organizing resistance into social movements. In E. Tuck & K. W. Yang (Eds.), *Youth resistance research and theories of change* (pp. 71-81). New York, NY: Routledge.

Orr, D. (2004). *Earth in mind: On education, environment, and the human prospect*. Washington, DC: First Island Press.

Radina, R. (2018). Resistance as an act of love: Remember your roots. *Currere Exchange Journal, 2*(1), 53-58.

Radina, R., Schwartz, T., Ross, G., Aronson, B., Albright-Willis, J., Wallace, M., & Norval, B. (2018). A space for us too: Using youth participatory action research to center youth voices. *School-University-Community Partnerships, 11*(4), 122-139.

Rodríguez, L. F. (2018). The PRAXIS Project: Participatory research advocating for excellence in schools. In J. Ayala, J. Cammarota, M. I. Berta-Ávila, M. Rivera, L. F. Rodríguez, & M. E. Torre (Eds.), *Par entremundos: A pedagogy of the Américas* (pp. 39-53). New York, NY: Peter Lang.

Sensoy, O., & DiAngelo, R. (2017). *Is everyone really equal?: An introduction to key concepts in social justice education.* New York, NY: Teachers College Press.

Taylor, S. R. (2018). *The body is not an apology: The power of radical self-love.* Oakland, CA: Berrett-Koehler Publishers, Inc.

www.ingramcontent.com/pod-product-compliance
Lightning Source LLC
Chambersburg PA
CBHW060803270326
41926CB00003B/79